STEVEN E. PHELAN

Startup Stories

Lessons for Everyday Entrepreneurs

First edition

ISBN: 978-0-578-72683-0

This book was professionally typeset on Reedsy.
Find out more at reedsy.com

Contents

Acknowledgement

I would like to sincerely thank the following people for making this book possible:

- Eric Koester, founder of the Creator Institute at Georgetown University
- Fellow students in my book writing class, particularly Anne Hoag, Hillary Lake, and Kevin Kurzendoerfer, who were gracious enough to provide interviews
- Jemiscoe Chambers-Black, my developmental editor
- My interview subjects
- Beta readers
- Noah Nihiser, proof reader and fact checker
- My daughter, Kathleen Phelan, for final editing
- Tasina Nitzschke, my muse and companion

Introduction

Steve Jobs is a hero of mine. I have taught a case on Apple Computer in my MBA strategy class for the past 25 years, following every twist and turn of the company's fortune. I became addicted to Apple products in my freshman year of college back in 1986. My dorm had purchased three Apple Mac Plus computers for student use, a not inconsiderable feat given the US$2,600 price tag per unit (about US$6,000 in 2020 dollars).

Of course, I had used other computers before, such as the TRS-80, released in 1977, and destined to become the most popular retail computer of its time. I had also used other machines that my friends owned - an Apple II, a Vic 20, a Commodore 64. What made the Mac unique was its beauty, its elegance, its aesthetic. Steve Jobs did not invent the mouse, the graphic user interface, or WYSIWYG (what you see is what you get). His particular genius was integrating these elements into a cohesive whole. The transition from an ugly box with a command-line interface, buggy software, and indifferent graphics to a Mac was magical for me. Apple was, and still is, a design company first and a technology company second. And Steve Jobs was its designer in chief. Unbeknownst to me at the time, he was also ousted from Apple in 1985, only to return in 1997.

Steve Jobs checks most of the boxes for the quintessential entrepreneur. Quintessential because he started Apple in his garage, assembled a team, created a product, raised capital to scale the business, and made money — a lot of money. He also took risks. The Mac division was essentially a startup within a startup. Jobs starved the successful Apple II product of talent and resources, throwing all his efforts into the Macintosh. His first effort, the Apple Lisa was a flop, but he hit a home run with the Apple Mac, not least because of his brilliant 1984 Superbowl ad comparing IBM to big brother. His return to Apple in 1997 was the stuff of legend with iconic products such as the iMac, iPod, iTunes, iPhone, and iPad being launched following his homecoming.

The Reality

Steve Jobs may be the quintessential entrepreneur, but he is not a typical entrepreneur. Over 500,000 businesses are started in the United States each month, but only around 300 of those will raise venture capital,[1] less than 1 in 1000. Of the roughly 17 million companies with employees, only 5,600 companies have an annual revenue above $1 billion per year, or about 3 in 10,000. Around 70-80% of those in self-employment do not employ anyone at all.[2]

Yet over 400,000 college students in the United States have taken at least one course in entrepreneurship,[3] even though the rate of self-employment has been falling for decades. In 1994, for instance, 12% of the US workforce listed their primary occupation as self-employed. In 2015, the number was 10%.[4] At the same time, the gig economy has been growing, with up to 27% of working age Americans receiving some or all of their income from independent work, including selling products, providing services, and renting assets.[5]

Are these students on a fool's errand? Are they chasing Jobs? I think there is a certain cachet to calling yourself an entrepreneur. You are a maverick, a risk-taker, ambitious, driven. It certainly makes a nice story to tell family and friends about why you are not working for a Fortune 500 company. However, the odds are stacked against you becoming the next Steve Jobs or Elon Musk, people I call super entrepreneurs.

I have also had my share of students telling me they are starting a business because they want to choose their own hours and go on vacation whenever they want. Autonomy is listed as the number one reason people enter self-employment, ranked even higher than getting rich. Unfortunately, there is no free lunch. Self-employed workers tend to work longer hours for less pay and benefits.[6] On the upside, they also have the highest job satisfaction of any job classification.

Economists like to tell a joke about two economists walking down a street. One casually remarks, "There's a $100 bill lying on the sidewalk over there." To which the colleague retorts, without looking, "No, there's not." What makes this funny to economists is that opportunities for easy money do not last very long. While many people aspire to be a billionaire, there are only about 600 billionaires in the United States, and 2,000 in the entire world.[7] That is 1 billionaire for every 4 million people on the planet! Billionaires are worth a lot, but they are also very rare.

Leveling Up in Entrepreneurship

I have been teaching entrepreneurship for 20 years. I have also worked (and lived) beside practicing entrepreneurs and dabbled in a few entrepreneurial ventures myself. I have known entrepreneurs who have gone broke and some who provided a decent standard of living for their families for 50 years. I have known others who had annual revenues in excess of $10 million, and a few who sold their businesses for over $100 million. This book is about sharing the stories of these entrepreneurs with those embarking on their own entrepreneurial journeys.

I like to picture entrepreneurship as a series of levels, like a video game. Doing so allows me to cast the widest possible net on entrepreneurial activity, from the simplest to the most advanced, and suggest habits you need to take your business to the next level. This book, then, is for every entrepreneur, including contractors, small business owners, and people who might not even consider themselves entrepreneurs in the traditional sense. It rejects the notion that unless you are striving to be a billionaire, you are not a 'real' entrepreneur. By the same token, it is very difficult to become a billionaire. This book will also demonstrate the challenges in going from one level of entrepreneurship to the next. It is good to set goals, but it is also good to know what level of effort it will take to achieve those goals.

The lower levels include the most common types of entrepreneurs. At the first level (Level 1) is *personal entrepreneurship*, the task of managing your own human capital over the span of your career, which may involve moving into and out of self-employment at different periods. In fact, around 40% of American workers will be self-employed at some stage in their careers.[8] It also includes intrapreneurship, that is, acting entrepreneurially within paid employment for others. Around 6.5% of workers in the United States label themselves as intrapreneurs at any given time.[9]

Level 2 is about *nascent entrepreneurs.* A nascent entrepreneur is anyone in the process of founding (or birthing) a business. Over 17% of Americans between the ages of 18 and 64 indicated they were starting or running a new business in 2019.[10] I divide this category into two groups: embryonic entrepreneurs are those wanting to start a business but have yet to earn revenue, while emerging entrepreneurs, are post-revenue but pre-profits.

Level 3 is about *lifestyle entrepreneurs.* Lifestyle entrepreneurs prefer to work for themselves rather than someone else and may not have profit maximization as their primary aim. Lifestyle entrepreneurs can be part-time or full-time, so self-employment can act as a complement to, or substitute for, paid employment. Virtual entrepreneurs are a growing sub-category of lifestyle entrepreneurs. These entrepreneurs are capable of growing considerable businesses with the aid of modern information technology while still managing to work from home with no employees.

Level 4 is the domain of *employer entrepreneurs*. The Global Entrepreneurship Monitor (GEM) uses the payment of wages as the dividing line between business owners and nascent entrepreneurs. According to GEM, around 10% of the adult population are established business owners who have been paying wages to themselves and others for longer than 42 months. Many of these operations are family businesses, and we will consider the unique challenges of working with family members. The World Bank reports that only 2.5% of those in the US workforce have hired non-family employees on a continuous basis to work for them, and 89% of all enterprises in the US have fewer than 20 employees.[11] So being an employer entrepreneur is quite a select group, facing some select challenges.

On Level 5, we encounter *growth entrepreneurs*. We examine expansionary entrepreneurs, who carefully add locations or products over time, and gazelle entrepreneurs, who seek to grow quickly and aspire to be the next Facebook or Google. Firms in the latter category are seeking to grow at double, if not triple, digit rates. They often seek to dominate a winner-takes-all or winner-takes-most industry with scalable technology.

Level 6 houses the *super entrepreneurs*, or what those in the trade call 'unicorns.' Unicorns are firms with private valuations of $1 billion or more. We approach this discussion for two angles. The first perspective examines the maverick nature of many of these entrepreneurs, a trait that might have helped them navigate the world in different ways. The second perspective considers what it takes to become a 'hero' entrepreneur, that is, one who is lionized by the business press.

The book ends with a final level dedicated to *artificial entrepreneurs*.

It explores how intelligent machines might complement entrepreneurs in their work. It also speculates on whether computers might one day displace human entrepreneurs as their level of intelligence grows to meet, and ultimately, exceed that of its human creators.

What to Expect

At each level, there is a discussion on the advantages of pursuing that particular type of entrepreneurship, the challenges that come with trying to make it work, and some ways an entrepreneur might develop to be successful at that level. The book is designed so that each level builds on the insights from the previous level, but it is also possible to jump right into the level you are interested in and start learning from there.

There are (at least) three things that I hope that you, the reader, will take away from this book. First, there are many ways to be an entrepreneur, most of which do not involve aspiring to be a billionaire. Second, you will have a road map of the type of skills and habits that you will need to develop to succeed at your desired level. As the great Yogi Berra said, "If you don't know where you're going, you might wind up somewhere else." Third, I hope that you will gain an appreciation that leveling up in entrepreneurship is hard work. In fact, Joe Colopy, who sold his company for $200 million in 2015, advises nascent entrepreneurs that "going from zero to $1 million in revenue will be the hardest thing you will ever do in your life."

The good news is that the odds of being a successful entrepreneur are higher than the odds of playing professional sports. As we saw earlier, up to 27% of US workers make at least part of their income from self-employment. That is millions of people making it work. I am confident that, with a little advice, you can too.

I

The Personal Entrepreneur

We are all capable of entrepreneurial behavior because we all possess resources, even if those resources are just our brain, body, and time. Choosing to consciously deploy our personal resources in search of valued outcomes makes us personal entrepreneurs.

Career Entrepreneurs

I distinctly recall a conversation with my parents when I was 16 years old. It went something like, "We can't afford to keep you. You need to drop out of school and get a job." This came as a major shock to me. We had never discussed careers or family finances before. I had never been asked to work even so much as a part-time job up to that point. It was also a minor tragedy. I was good at school and dropping out would close off a lot of options.

But I also understood where my parents were coming from. Neither had finished high school themselves. My mother left school after ninth grade to work in a clothing factory. My father left after tenth grade. As was the tradition at that time, my mother had stopped work when she got married, so my father's single income supported a family of five. At that time, the legal age you could leave school was 15 so, as the oldest son, I was quite capable of contributing to the family.

In a panic, I launched into full-blown career search mode. My school offered one-week "work experience" opportunities. It was normal for kids to try one or two occupations through these modestly paid internships. I tried three. The first was selling pianos and organs at the local music store. Unfortunately, I was a nerd with few social skills, so I sucked at sales. It did not help that the full-time salesperson warned me not to sell anything that carried a commission for him. I recall a family coming into the store who asked me to demonstrate the most expensive organ on the floor while the real salesperson was out to lunch. Terrified, I kept explaining that we would have to wait for my colleague to return. After waiting for 30 minutes, they left in a very dissatisfied state after cursing my incompetence.

The second paid internship was working for the local ambulance service. My father taught first aid for the Red Cross and he was able to secure me a week of work experience through this connection. I liked it. A lot of the time involved sitting around waiting for jobs or transporting elderly patients. Occasionally, however, these periods were punctuated with emergencies, lights, sirens, and high-speed driving - all very exciting for a 16-year-old boy! More importantly, I was helping people every day, which provided a high degree of job satisfaction. Many of the women in my family (my maternal grandmother and three aunts) had been in the nursing profession so helping the sick and elderly was in my blood.

The final placement was with the local television station, a highly sought-after slot, that unfortunately did not appeal to me in the least. I spent most of my time in the production department, assisting (or, more accurately, not getting in the way of) advertising shoots and live TV, including the local news, a variety show, and a cooking show. It would be an understatement to say how much the crew looked forward to eating the fabulous dishes from that show. I also went out with a news crew on location and observed the work of the video and sound editors. Overall, they were a wonderfully talented and personable group of individuals. At the end of the week, I met with the station manager, who chastised me for spending too much time in production and not seeing other parts of the station. He was even more incensed when I revealed that I did not think a life in television was for me. He cited the huge list of applicants for an internship, who would have done almost anything for the chance I was given. For my part, I had discovered something else that I was not cut out for.

The most attractive proposition turned out to be the Royal Australian Navy (RAN). At the time, in 1983, the RAN paid a small senior year scholarship for those accepted as officer candidates at the Naval Academy. They would also fund my college education in exchange for four years of active duty service. It was a good fit. I was already a military history buff, not least because my grandfather had served in the Second World War on the hospital ship *MS Wanganella*. Each year, on Anzac Day (the Australian equivalent of Memorial Day), veterans would march in a parade in every city and town in Australia, with each unit having its own contingent marching behind a banner. The Melbourne march was televised, and my father would proudly point out the banner of the veterans from the *Wanganella* and pass around his father's service medals. The Navy checked a lot of boxes - an income, an occupation respected by my parents, and a college education. It gave me a goal to pursue for the next two years of my life.

So, what does all this have to do with entrepreneurship? Plenty, as it turns out. The bottom line is that we are all custodians of our own *human capital*. Human capital is the economic value we derive from our stock of skills and experience. According to Investopedia, "it includes assets like education, training, intelligence, skills, health, and other things of value to employers such as loyalty and punctuality." Some things we are born with: intelligence, height, and general health. Other aspects of our human capital can be developed. I can learn to be more punctual or program a computer, for instance.

A capitalist is someone who invests capital in the hope of future gain. We normally think of capital as financial capital (i.e. money). But there are many different types of capital. Physical capital is another example, which includes buildings, land, and equipment. Social capital is another term in vogue. It refers to the social connections that you have developed over your life. Social capital is a form of knowledge, it is *know-who* and complements other forms of knowledge like *know-*

5

what and *know-how*. Knowledge, in turn, forms an important part of our human capital.

One thing we know for sure is that the future is uncertain. That is why capital is invested in the 'hope' or 'expectation' of gain rather than a guaranteed return. Even the most secure investment in US treasury bonds carries the risk that the government will default on its debt obligation. The US has so far avoided this dubious honor, but many countries throughout history have defaulted on their debt obligations. Similarly, we make an investment in our human capital in the belief that there will be a future return. However, there are no guarantees, and even the safest job, such as a tenured college professor, is subject to elimination. Nothing is certain in life except death and taxes, as the saying goes.

Luckily, a lot of capital is *fungible*, that is, it has multiple uses. As such, we can apply our money, equipment, or knowledge to a range of activities. Writing and arithmetic are highly fungible skills that can be used in a range of occupations and endeavors. Similarly, cash or even a cash register can be deployed to many different uses. On the other hand, economists use the term 'asset specificity' to refer to capital that cannot easily be deployed to other uses.

Given that I can develop and deploy my human capital across a range of activities, which activity (or mix of activities) should I choose? Largely, this will depend on my preferences, that is my likes and dislikes, and the trade-offs between these preferences. As we saw earlier, I did not like the sales job, I liked emergency services tolerably well, and I could not see myself working in television. But it is not just about what I like. I also have to consider the compensation for those activities, the investment of time and effort required to achieve a certain level of success, the risk that I won't get a return on my investment, the fungibility (or other options) for my investment, and the amount of time left over for other things I value, such as leisure, sleep, and raising a family. At the age of sixteen, I chose the navy as the best balance of all these factors. Was it a completely informed decision? Certainly not. I had limited life and career experiences at that stage. But it was a conscious choice, nonetheless. The conscious choice to invest my time and build my human capital towards naval service in the hope of realizing uncertain, but valued, outcomes was an entrepreneurial decision. Without knowing it, I became a career entrepreneur, managing my human capital.

Advantages

Flexibility is the hallmark of a career entrepreneur. A career entrepreneur is not bound by arbitrary categories like employed or unemployed. Unpaid work, engaging in stints of self-employment, or pursuing more education can be all be valid life choices, provided you are following what appears to be the path to greatest happiness at the time. In doing so, you will be able to adapt to the vagaries of changing preferences and opportunities.

Being a career entrepreneur is thus the safest way to experience entrepreneurship. There is no pressure to engage in all or nothing thinking like, "I have to quit my job to be a real entrepreneur" or "My idea is not innovative enough for the big time." As a career entrepreneur, events can occur on your own schedule, at a scale that makes you physically, financially, and psychologically comfortable.

Challenges

We, as humans, tend to get too comfortable and, unless we are challenging ourselves, might not reach our fullest potential. Of course, there is no score card at the end of the game of life that awards a low grade for failing to be the best we can be. However, many people seem

7

to be interested in life hacks that will jolt them out of complacency and help them achieve more of their life goals. Similarly, life coaches often challenge their clients to move "out of their comfort zones."

It is also true that much of our life is determined by chance - the time and place we are born, our genetic inheritance, our parents. It may surprise you to learn that I did not go into the Navy after high school. Instead, I balked at the final interview and, with the advice of a local guidance counselor, attended the University of Melbourne. That turned out to be one of the most consequential decisions of my life. What I did not realize at the time, being the first in my family to attend college, was that Melbourne was one of the top fifty universities in the world. There was no way I could have imagined the first-class education that I would receive in psychology — an education that has carried me on to other career successes throughout my life.

While my decision to turn down the Navy and go to a traditional college killed my chances of being an admiral, it opened a lot more possibilities, including the possibility of becoming a professor. Every one of us can look back and consider the road not taken. Each decision we make in our career locks us into a certain set of future choices and locks us out of others. As we spend more time going down a certain path, our choices tend to become more limited.

An entrepreneurial journey is also likely to be influenced by child-hood experiences. I asked Kevin Kurzendoerfer, the former Chief Operating Officer of an online grocery store, whether entrepreneurs were born or made. He gave an interesting answer. "I think early childhood and through...elementary school you decide things you like and don't like and start doing more of the things you like." He gave the example of his two sons, one who is analytical and the other more creative. "Ask [the first child] to create something or draw somebody and he freezes up but give him a math problem and he's off to the races." According to Kevin, our innate tendencies influence how you are treated by your parents, further reinforcing your development. "So the one that likes art, we are funneling him into more art stuff and more creative opportunities," he said.

Ways to Develop

By this point, some of you might be thinking, "I don't have what it takes. I was not born in an affluent family; I have the wrong personality for this. I'm just not that lucky." Believing that you are at the mercy of outside forces is an example of what psychologists call an external locus of control. People with an external locus of control believe they can do little to influence their situation. They tend to drift in life, believing that their choices have little bearing on how things turn out. Conversely, those with a strong internal locus of control believe they can control or influence the world around them.

I think the truth lies somewhere in the middle. The controversial Canadian psychologist, Jordan Peterson, sparked a mass following among young men, many of whom were still living with their parents, by exhorting them to "make your bed." His argument was that you have almost total control of the state of your bedroom and so you have no excuse for leaving it in chaos. His larger point was there is almost certainly something we can do in almost every situation. Biology is not destiny.

If entrepreneurship is about making deliberate choices about how to deploy your time and resources, then taking personal responsibility lies at the heart of entrepreneurship. Personal responsibility is not something you have or do not have. It is something that can be developed. Small life hacks like "make your bed" can remind you that you have more control over a situation than you think you have.

Another hack that I recommend is "If not you, then who?" How many times have you walked by a trash can where someone has failed in their attempt to put a small item in the rather large opening at the top? How many times have you walked by an empty coffee pot at work and thought, "Someone should make a fresh pot of coffee?" Each time something like this happens, try to ask yourself, "If not me, then who?" Don't avoid the situation, don't pretend it's not there, don't wait for someone else to do it. Pick up the trash and put it in the trash can. Make a new pot of coffee. Once you have mastered these small habits you can begin to work on larger challenges.

Ultimately, the goal is getting to the point where *carpe diem*, Latin for 'seize the day', becomes your motto. I am a procrastinator. I know this about myself. My natural tendency is to embrace the slacker creed, "Never do today what you can put off to tomorrow." One of the ways I motivate myself is to create arbitrary deadlines. I set my alarm for 5 a.m. each weekday morning so I can work on this book. There is no reason I must be up at 5 a.m. other than to signal to myself that I am already making a sacrifice by waking up early, so I may as well just write. Another technique is to publicly commit to a deadline. I find the potential humiliation of not meeting an arbitrary deadline to be an effective motivator to perform. This, of course, is just me. You need to find your own hacks that work for you. The bottom line is that being entrepreneurial means taking charge of your life, to create more steering and less drifting.

Kenny is a career entrepreneur

Kenny Kury was raised in Amarillo, Texas. Like many high school students, he had no idea what he wanted to do when he graduated so he drifted into the restaurant business, where he eventually found himself managing an ice cream store. The job exposed him to many different skills, including managing staff, keeping an eye on the books, and improving processes.

Married at the age of 20, he supported his wife while she finished college. He then decided to attend college himself. Kenny found bookkeeping to be one of the most enjoyable parts of being a manager, so he decided to major in accounting. After graduation, he went to work for a public accounting firm for a few years, where he audited the books for many companies, including the local ABC affiliate. Following a merger, his Amarillo accounting office was closed, and he applied for a job as an accounting manager at a local TV station, where he was able to combine his management know-how from the ice cream job and his accounting knowledge from the auditing job.

After five years at the TV station, he moved to South Padre Island, following his divorce and a general dissatisfaction with how the TV station treated its staff. Unsure of what he wanted to do, he ended up buying his parents' drapery business after they announced their intention to retire. As Kenny put it, "I wasn't as emotionally attached to the business as my parents were. It could have been any business because I approached it as a businessperson." Kenny ran the drapery business for almost ten years, expanding its operations to include an in-house upholstery business run by a talented employee that he recruited from a former sub-contractor. During this period, he completed an MBA and started a small consulting practice setting up accounting and point of sale systems. He was also certified in business valuation.

After a decade, attracted by the prospect of an academic lifestyle, he sold the business and applied to join the PhD program in Management at Boston College in 2000, at the age of 38. Graduating in 2006, he started as a tenure-track professor in entrepreneurship at St. Joseph's University in Philadelphia, where he has remained to this day. His experiences in management and running a small business have been enormously helpful for his teaching and research. His exposure to Jesuit philosophies also ignited an interest in social entrepreneurship, which is the use of entrepreneurial skills to pursue a social mission, like the alleviation of poverty or disease eradication.

Kenny's career arc is an excellent illustration of many of the points that were raised earlier. The first is how someone can move in and out of different forms of employment. Kenny describes himself as being on his fifth or sixth career, with each career benefiting from the knowledge gained in previous roles. The second point is that most careers tend to be a combination of steering and drifting. By his own admission, Kenny drifted into the restaurant industry after high school. However, he was more deliberate in his choice of accounting, based on his management experience and interest in bookkeeping. Although he did not move to South Padre Island to take over a drapery business, there was a deliberate choice to leverage his business skills to acquire the business when his parents announced their intention to retire. In doing so, he was behaving entrepreneurially, making a deliberate decision to apply his human capital to attempt to realize financial gain from a going concern. Later, he made the deliberate choice to move to a job with an attractive mix of benefits and worked for five to six years to acquire the qualifications (i.e. productive resources or human capital) needed to enter his newly chosen profession. He is now reaping the benefits of that investment.

Summary

An entrepreneur in popular culture is an innovative, risk-taker that aggressively pursues growth in the hope of a big pay day. In this chapter, we have introduced a different type of entrepreneur, the career entrepreneur, who manages the human capital of just one person. However, the same elements of choice and uncertainty are present in both types of entrepreneurs. An investment in education or training will probably pay off but there are no guarantees. This is no different than an investment in technology or the stock market, although the size of the investment may differ.

The key lesson of this chapter is to approach as many decisions as possible in a proactive manner. Not everything is within our control, and not every decision will work out the way we intended. Along the way, there will be happy accidents and unforeseen tragedies. At the end of the day, however, being an entrepreneur means taking control of your life and believing that a set of conscious decisions will eventually lead you to a place you want to be.

Intrapreneurs

I n 2018 and 2019, I held the title of Provost Fellow for Academic Innovation, where I was placed in charge of overseeing new initiatives for the Chief Academic Officer of the university, including new programs, new delivery channels, new technology, and new processes. One such initiative involved creating a customer relationship management (CRM) system. Students were calling the admissions office with specific questions about academic programs (such as nursing or business). The admission officers were not experts on specific programs, so they needed to refer these questions to academic departments. Unfortunately, following the referral, they had no way of knowing whether the student received an answer or ended up enrolling in the program. Anecdotal evidence suggested that questions from prospective students were not being answered by departments. I suggested we should build a CRM system to track these inquiries.

A CRM system essentially allows an organization to track inquiries from their customers and potential customers (in this case prospective students), maintain a history of interactions, and allow customer-facing groups to communicate with these groups with the knowledge of past interactions. For example, a prospective student who asks about transfer credits for the nursing program might receive a follow-up reminder about the application deadline. If the same student called the admissions office, the admission officer would have a full record of past communications, such as questions that were asked (and answered), emails sent (and opened), attendance at campus events like a campus tour or open house, and phone calls made to the university.

Fortunately, there are many technological platforms available to deliver these services, ranging from off-the-shelf solutions, systems specific to the higher education industry, or even fully customized platforms. However, selecting an appropriate technology is only part of the challenge. The selected technology must also work alongside existing systems, processes, and procedures within the university; the users of the technology have to be incentivized to use the new system; and the university needs to find the resources to buy, develop, deploy, and operate the system. An interdisciplinary task force comprising several academic deans and academic support professionals (from admissions, enrollment management, and marketing) was assembled under my leadership to address these challenges.

Five weeks later, we were able to place a button on the top right corner of the university home page that allowed prospective students to 'request info' from a specific program. Based on the program selected, the question was routed to four different people in the department who operated the program, with instructions to reply to the query within 48 hours. Questions and replies were logged in a database and academic deans were given weekly reports on questions that were pending beyond the 48-hour deadline. Within one month, virtually 100% of all inquiries were answered within 48 hours. The admissions office was able to access the contact details of these prospective students and created a communication plan to encourage them to apply before our deadlines. Enrollments were up the following year.

Being an *intrapreneur* is another way we can exercise personal entrepreneurship. An intrapreneur is an employee within an existing organization who develops something new, and hopefully valuable. The Global Entrepreneurship Monitor, which tracks total entrepreneurial activity (TEA) in fifty countries, includes a category for employee entrepreneurial activity (EEA). In 2019, in the United States, more than 6% of adults 18 to 64 reported being involved in employee entrepreneurial activity. The number was more than 8% in the United Kingdom and Australia.[12]

Advantages for intrapreneurs

Clearly, one of the advantages of being an intrapreneur is lower risk. Instead of putting your own financial capital on the line, you get to use the financial resources of your employer. You also continue to draw a steady paycheck, whether your ideas are working or not. You are also not alone. Working in a larger organization means you have access to specialists from many different departments.

Employers also value people who can solve unstructured problems. An unstructured problem is one in which there are no preexisting routines or policies in the organization to handle a situation. In other words, something new must be devised. Traditional MBA students are very good at solving structured problems, that is, problems where the data and technique are given. However, they are less proficient at solving unstructured problems (according to surveys of companies that hire MBA graduates).[13] This, in turn, makes these skills rare and thus valuable to senior management, which may open promotion opportunities.

Finally, becoming a corporate entrepreneur (or intrapreneur) is a good way to prepare yourself for future self-employment. Seeing a better way of doing things that has been overlooked (or actively rejected) by one's employer has often been the motivation to launch a new enterprise. However, as we will see in our closing case, it is also possible to hold an entrepreneurial spirit for decades and positively contribute to the life of any organization you find yourself in.

Challenges for intrapreneurs

One of the reasons entrepreneurs are so motivated to succeed is because they have what economists call 'high-powered incentives,' that is, compensation is directly linked to the size of their success (or failure). As an entrepreneur, you get to keep all the cash you generate after you have covered your costs. You also have the option of selling your stake to the highest bidder and 'cashing out' for a lump sum. Employees, on the other hand, tend to have low-powered incentives. They get paid the same whether they add something to the bottom line or not. This, in turn, reduces their incentive to innovate. Forward-looking companies have attempted to address this problem by offering bonuses or stock options, but most employees do not have access to these programs. So, as an intrapreneur, you might struggle to motivate yourself and others in your organization to change because you don't directly benefit from the value you create (although arguably you benefit indirectly by helping your organization survive, or even flourish).

Another challenge is that large organizations are often built for efficiency rather than innovation, and the best way to be efficient is not to change anything! I learned this lesson several decades ago while working with a technology transfer team at Texas Instruments. The team was responsible for upgrading the semiconductor production lines with new computer chip technology. It was a constant struggle with the plant managers to shut the line down to install new equipment, as those managers were rewarded for continuous operation. Of course, without new technology, the company would not stay competitive for long. As a result, the issue had to be wrangled by senior management every time a shutdown for an upgrade was required. There is a fine line to walk between being an effective intrapreneur and being perceived as a troublemaker. Senior management support is critical here as many barriers can be overcome with the right backing. However, in some cases, senior management have been known to disavow innovators if they start generating serious resistance.

Ways to develop

The best thing you can do to develop yourself as an intrapreneur is to work on your individual entrepreneurial orientation. In the 1980s, entrepreneurship researchers hypothesized that some organizations were more entrepreneurial than others. Subsequent studies found that not only did organizations vary in their entrepreneurial orientation, or EO as it came to be known, but that organizations with higher EOs also tended to perform better.[14] Amazingly, these results seemed to hold not only for small for-profit firms, but also for large firms and non-profit organizations, like churches and schools.[15] These results have been replicated around the world.

Individual entrepreneurial orientation (or IEO) is the notion that individuals, as well as organizations, can develop and display entrepreneurial behaviors that correlate with personal success.[16] Entrepreneurial orientation has traditionally been divided into three underlying dimensions: proactiveness, innovativeness, and risk-taking.

Proactiveness

Proactive behavior involves acting in advance of a future situation. Proactive people actively initiate change rather than adapt or react to it. In my view, proactivity is the single most important entrepreneurial behavior after taking personal responsibility.

Sam Altman is the former CEO of the highly successful accelerator, Y Combinator, which helped to launch household names like AirBnB and DropBox. Altman also co-founded Open AI with Elon Musk. When asked what he looks for in a founder, he mentions that some founders are fast and others slow. Fast founders respond to important emails very quickly. Everything is done with a sense of urgency. In his experience, investing in a company with a fast founder is a better bet. Research seems to back up his intuition. Successful companies tend to be up and running in three months, while less successful companies average ten months. The reason, of course, is that achieving results requires action. You can talk all you like about your business idea, but you will see no results until you commit time and money and start making things happen.

Can we learn to be more proactive? I would argue yes. In the previous chapter, I argued that you could cultivate personal responsibility in small ways, such as taking the trash out or refilling the coffee pot, rather than waiting on someone else to do it. Proactivity is a similar idea, but the actions are taken *in advance* of a future situation. Thus, a proactive person must mentally project the current state of the world into the future, anticipate an issue, then deal with it in the present.

Catching a plane is a good example. We tend to adjust the time we leave for the airport depending on the type of flight (international or domestic) and the time of day (it will take longer to get there in rush hour traffic). We then adjust our departure time accordingly. We can train ourselves to develop the same mindset with our work. It is reasonably safe to assume that if a problem occurs a few times in a row then it will likely happen again. For instance, in the CRM example above, questions from prospective students were routinely not being answered. It was safe to assume the situation would keep on happening unless something was changed. So, the easiest way to become proactive is to look for patterns. Look for problems that keep on occurring and then take responsibility to do something about it.

Innovativeness

What to do about a problem is the domain of innovativeness. Creativity refers to the production of novel or useful ideas, while innovation is the successful implementation of those ideas. So being innovative is not just about coming up with a novel solution to a problem but also realizing the idea in practice.

Novelty in this sense does not have to mean 'new to the world.' Implementing a solution that is 'new to your organization' or 'new to your department' is also being innovative. As such, Google can be your friend. It is not difficult to do a little digging on how others are solving a problem. There are millions of organizations in the world and is unlikely that your institution is the only one facing a given problem. Comparing yourself to others is formally known as benchmarking, and it is something that literally anyone can practice and develop over time. There is often no need to reinvent the wheel.

In my experience, there is often more creativity required in making something work in context than generating the original idea itself. In the CRM example above, the idea of putting a button on the home page is not very original, but making it work within my organization in a given period with a limited budget is another matter. Execution is a creative act, sometimes requiring what the French call *bricolage*, or the cobbling together of a solution from things that happen to be laying around. As such, solutions often come from connecting existing resources together in new ways, by finding new associations.[17]

I sometimes hear people say, "But I don't have a creative bone in my body." While there is undoubtedly a genetic component to creativity, there are also ways to develop your skills in this area. One of the easiest ways is networking. Organizations typically work in silos. The accounting department spends most of its day with other accounting staff, the marketing department with other marketing people. Deliberately trying to get out of your silo is what networking is about. Program yourself to take opportunities to meet other people, particularly those from other departments. Ask them about what they do, what their problems are, what resources they have available. Then, when the time comes to make associations or connections among existing resources, you will have a rich pool of knowledge to draw from: "Oh, Mary in marketing can do this, and Paul in accounting has a system that can do that."

Risk-Taking

From some reason, my mind always conjoins *crazy* and *risk-taker* together, as in "that crazy risk-taker just went over Niagara Falls in a barrel again." However, research has shown that successful entrepreneurs see the same risks as the next person.[18] However, instead of avoiding risk, they seek to manage risk, take calculated risks, or even de-risk a situation.[19] At the end of the day, being future-oriented and innovative requires living with uncertainty.

A century ago, the economist Frank Knight drew a sharp distinction between risk and uncertainty.[20] Risk, according to Knight, is something where you can calculate the odds of something happening. For instance, I know when I roll a pair of dice that I have a 1 in 6 chance of a 7 appearing, while a 2 will only occur on 1 in 36 rolls. I can calculate these odds mathematically and empirically (by tabulating the outcome of many rolls). Uncertainty, on the other hand, is resistant to probability. Something that is new to the world has never happened before, so it is impossible to predict the outcome based on past results. The iPad is a case in point. In some ways, the iPad is just a big iPhone or a small laptop, but the exact configuration was completely new. Industry commentators were skeptical about the need for the item, but Steve Jobs believed there was a demand out there, and he acted on his intuition. History showed that Jobs was correct.

The issue, then, is not whether we can control risk but whether we can learn to live with uncertainty, and develop a tolerance for ambiguity. The first thing is to embrace failure. The top hitter in the Baseball Hall of Fame, Ty Cobb, had a batting average of 0.366, meaning he was able to hit a pitch and advance to first base 366 times for every 1000 pitches. In other words, he failed 634 times in a thousand. The upshot is that not every idea is going to work, even with the best preparation. Recognizing this fact goes a long way towards developing a tolerance for ambiguity.

Thinking experimentally is one way to mitigate the effects of failure when they occur. An experimental mindset encourages making small bets, seeing if a concept works, adjusting as required, and failing fast if something is not going to work. From this perspective, it is better to trial a new product or process in one location for a limited time than spend millions on a national roll out that fails spectacularly. A failed experiment that saves millions is a win.

Anne is an intrapreneur

Bill Daniels was a legendary entrepreneur in the 20th century. A former Air Force pilot with little formal education, he started a cable television company in Casper, Wyoming in 1954. He would go on to own and operate hundreds of systems across the country, becoming a billionaire in the process. But this story is not about Bill. It is about a 26-year-old employee of Bill's named Anne Hoag.

Anne grew up in the Midwest and attended the University of Michigan, where she graduated with a degree in film and video studies in 1981. After a few years as a talent/broadcast coordinator with the Leo Burnett Company in Chicago, she landed a job with Bill's company, Daniel & Associates, as an Operations Management Trainee in July

1987. Within six months, with no formal management training, she was made an acting general manager at Cablevision!

It turns out Bill had a formula of sorts. Following the deregulation of the cable industry in 1984, he had proceeded to acquire small community cable companies across the country. He would then install a new general manager who would expand the channel offerings, improve customer service, and raise prices. Then, he would flip the now highly profitable company to a larger entity like Comcast. I say a formula of sorts because every flip was different. Different markets required different programming, and often the price increases were vigorously resisted by locals. An effective general manager was often the difference that made the whole thing work.

Anne admits she was very green at the time. "I don't know if you noticed, but I don't know much," she said to her mentor, a trusted lieutenant of Bill Daniels. But she was a ferociously quick learner recalling, "[My mentor] somehow trusted me and believed in me, and that was really empowering." He also showed her how to develop her personal entrepreneurial orientation. Her Midwest upbringing had taught her to "follow the rules...follow instructions." At Daniel & Associates, Bill created a culture that encouraged his staff to be innovative and take risks. "I just had so much freedom to try stuff out. I was encouraged to try things...we don't know what these new channels are, but go ahead and try them out," recalled Anne, "I was socialized into this kind of bias toward action." Looking back, more than 30 years later, Anne opines, "I would never in a million years have been an entrepreneur except for the way I was socialized in this company. I didn't know another industry where a young woman with my experience could have been given such an interesting opportunity."

Anne left the cable industry in 1992 to pursue a PhD in mass media at Michigan State University. Following graduation, she accepted a job at Penn State University, where she recently marked 20 years of service. Beyond consulting, Anne never started her own company, but her intrapreneuring did not end when she became a professor. "We've got 100,000 students and 24 campuses. And it is super bureaucratic. But it is really fun to test it and see what I can do," said Anne.

Inspired by her experiences in the cable industry, Anne went on to co-found the intercollegiate minor in entrepreneurship at Penn State in 2012. "We wanted to start an entrepreneurship program," she said, "but we [also] wanted it to be a minor, because you need to be in mechanical engineering or architecture or journalism to know what the problems are that need to be solved." The program was innovative and risky. "It's the only program at Penn State that's not in an academic college," said Anne. "I still can't believe it worked." But her few years with the cable industry, decades earlier, had taught her to persevere and "understand the power of being uncomfortable." Today, the program is the third largest minor in the Penn State system.

Summary

Back in 1988, Professor Bill Gartner, then an assistant professor at Georgetown University, defined entrepreneurship as the creation of new organizations, and encouraged researchers to focus on the process by which new organizations came into existence. This tended to focus attention on the startup as the place where 'true' entrepreneurship occurs.

Today, however, entrepreneurship is conceived as a method that can be practiced in a wide range of contexts. One such context involves using the entrepreneurial method within an existing organization. While the risks and rewards may not be as extreme, intrapreneurs share many similarities with entrepreneurs in other contexts, including a bias for action, a focus on innovation, and a tolerance for ambiguity and failure.

The ability to solve novel, unstructured problems is a valuable skill that also tends to be highly transferable between organizations. At the same time, mature organizations also resist change and innovation, and intrapreneurs may become frustrated without top management support, which may itself be fickle.

Some intrapreneurs may end up founding their own organizations if the situation becomes intolerable. Others, on the other hand, see navigating these obstacles as part of the challenge and elect to remain. Neither choice is inherently superior or 'more entrepreneurial.'

II

The Nascent Entrepreneur

A nascent entrepreneur is someone in the process of starting a business.
The word nascent comes from Latin for 'being born'.
Around 12% of American adults are in the process of birthing a business at any given time.

Embryonic Entrepreneurs

D r. Shirley Chao, a professor of biology at Fayetteville State University (FSU), made an intriguing discovery in her lab one day. She found that adding a little hemp flour to wheat flour killed or deformed insects trying to feed on the wheat. After experimenting with different proportions of flour, she found that when hemp flour comprised just 2% of the mixture it disabled 80-100% of the target insects!

It is a little-known fact that 5-10% of the stored grain in the United States (mostly corn and wheat) is lost to insects each year. To control these losses, farmers spend almost $1 billion on highly toxic pesticides to protect their crops after harvest. However, these chemicals are also toxic to humans, and there is evidence that there are dangerous health implications resulting from long-term exposure. Shirley's discovery that non-toxic hemp flour could act as an insecticide had the potential to improve the lives of farm workers and their families, while also protecting valuable crops.

Others agreed. In 2015, a group of business students wrote a business plan for CannaMix, as Shirley had titled her invention. The plan was submitted to the University of North Carolina's social entrepreneurship competition, competing against teams from all sixteen campuses in the UNC system, and won first place in the graduate division. Based on this positive feedback, Shirley worked with the university to patent her idea. In doing so, Shirley became an embryonic entrepreneur.

There are a lot of misconceptions about patents among inventors (and entrepreneurs). Simply put, a patent gives the inventor the right to exclude others from using an invention for a period of twenty years in exchange for fully disclosing how the invention works. A patent examiner examines the claims in a patent application to determine if there is something new. While those claims are being examined, the patent is said to be pending, with an average wait time of almost three years for a determination to be made. Shirley's patent was filed in March 2015 and awarded in October 2015.

Once a patent is granted, the inventor has the right to retrospectively sue anyone using the invention while it was pending. The inventor can also sue anyone else who infringes in the future. To avoid being sued, other parties typically agree to pay the inventor for the right to use the invention. These agreements are known as licenses and the payments are known as royalties. Often, royalties are structured as a percentage of revenue, so an inventor might receive 5-10% of the revenues from a product based on the invention.

Clearly, if no revenue is generated by the licensee then there are no royalty payments to the inventor. Another problem is an individual or corporation might consciously infringe on your patent knowing you lack the resources to defend your claim in court. Although 95% of patent claims are settled before entering a court room, it can easily take $1 million or more to 'have your day in court.' Even with the strongest claim, it is still a coin toss whether you will prevail, with the 18th century French writer Voltaire quipping, "I have been bankrupt twice in my life, once when I lost a lawsuit, and once when I won."

Today, inventors are most likely to work for large corporations and universities, trading a steady salary for the risks involved in making money from a patent. As a result, they end up 'assigning' their invention to their employer. FSU, like other campuses in the UNC system, allows inventors to have a share in the income derived from a patent. After the patent was granted, Shirley decided to start a company to commercialize her idea, with her company effectively licensing the patent back from the university (and herself). To date, she continues to work towards monetizing her invention.

Advantages

Being an embryonic entrepreneur is an exciting time. A decision has been made to launch a new business and steps are being taken to make that a reality. Exactly which steps are being taken varies by the type of business being started but might include:

- Applying for a patent, trademark, or copyright
- Seeking funding
- Investing your own money into the business
- Hiring employees or managers
- Asking financial institutions or other people for funding
- Establishing credit with suppliers
- Putting a startup team together
- Acquiring a business name, website, and phone number
- Purchasing, leasing, or renting major equipment
- Working full-time on the business
- Starting marketing or promotion activities
- Purchasing supplies
- Preparing a business plan and/or financial projections
- Registering a firm
- Reporting a sale
- Working on a model or prototype

Researchers have learned a lot about nascent entrepreneurs over the past two decades. They start by calling many people at random and asking them if they are in the process of starting a business. Those who say yes are then tracked over several years to see what happens. Data collection for the first of these studies, known as the Panel Study of Entrepreneurial Dynamics, was started in the United States in July 1998.[21]

As part of these studies, over 2,500 founders from the USA, China, Sweden, and Australia were asked about the sort of steps they undertook to get their business off the ground.[22] These are known as gestation activities. The good news is undertaking any two or three of the activities listed above was sufficient for a business to reach profitability within two years, and, like Shirley, around 80% of entrepreneurs continue to work in a full-time job while starting their new venture.[23]

Challenges

Being an embryonic entrepreneur can be a challenging time. There can be a steep learning curve for someone like Shirley with little experience in business, and it can sometimes feel like you are drinking from a fire hose. As a result, there is a constant worry about whether you are doing the right thing. This is compounded by the fact that you are often investing a lot of time and money into your idea without a guaranteed return. As an embryonic entrepreneur you have yet to generate revenue, let alone profit.

Another challenge is being overly attached to a vision of the way the business must run. I once had an embryonic entrepreneur present to my class about opening a high-end retail establishment. However, it turned out realizing her vision would require going $200,000 into debt and operating in an industry where she admitted to having little experience. The students quite reasonably pointed out that she might wish to start small, perhaps selling door-to-door, so she could build up industry experience and a client base. She left the room in tears, not prepared to see her dream shattered in this way. Later, she told me she had invested almost $70,000 in the idea already. While passion and perseverance are often seen as positive attributes for entrepreneurs, the same traits can also lead to tunnel vision about the best way to move forward.

However, the greatest challenge for embryonic entrepreneurs is probably inaction. Ideas are a dime a dozen and what really matters is execution. In the four-country study mentioned earlier, only about 10% of startups had a positive cash flow after 12 months, and 20% after two years. Around 50% of the entrepreneurs reported they were still working on their idea three years later, while 30% had given up. One of the reasons that so many entrepreneurs continue to work on their idea is that many of the gestation activities listed above do not require a large financial investment. Time (also known as 'sweat equity') is often the only investment required. This enables some budding entrepreneurs to drag out the process. At some point however, a significant investment is required, and, at that stage, the journey is ended for many.

Of course, this pattern clearly varies by industry. Scientific break-throughs, like CannaMix, often take many years to reach commercial viability, as the basic invention needs to be refined and optimized for large-scale production and distribution. For the average entrepreneur, however, opportunities can be fleeting and it pays to act rather than procrastinate.

Ways to develop

A lot of the lessons from earlier chapters can be applied to embryonic entrepreneurs. Being proactive and taking responsibility are crucial mindsets to develop. Only 15% of startups report only two or more gestation activities in a six-month period with enterprises reporting their first sales undertaking significantly more activities.[24] Making a conscious effort to work on several relevant gestation activities each month can greatly differentiate you from the average founder.

Experience can also be important. Research shows that successful entrepreneurs often have 10 or more years of industry experience before starting a business.[25] There is a reason for this. Industry experience provides a great deal of knowledge about how a business in your chosen field works. Simple things like how to find customers, price your product, hire and train employees, and deal with suppliers are skills that can usually be acquired by working in your chosen field. Entrepreneurs are well-advised to work for someone in the industry before starting a business. This can be seen most clearly in the construction trades where workers traditionally serve as apprentices and learn the trade by working for someone else. At some point, some proportion strike out on their own. Similarly, in the high-end retail example above, the students recommended going door-to-door for a period to learn about customers and their needs before investing large sums of money.

There are also substitutes for experience. Over the last 10 years, the idea of doing a 'lean startup' has taken the tech world by storm. First popularized by Eric Ries in his 2011 book *The Lean Startup*, the idea is to fail fast and fail frugally.[26] Many founders, particularly in the technology sector, have no real idea if there is a customer for their product as they tend to focus on building a workable technology first. Steve Blank, Ries' mentor at the University of California Berkeley, advises founders to 'get out of the building' and speak with at least 50 prospective customers.[27] If possible, founders should also build a cheap model or prototype, so customers have something tangible to react to.

If customers are not enthusiastic about an idea then a founder should 'pivot,' that is, make some changes to the initial concept so it is more appealing. In this approach, entrepreneurs are constantly being challenged to test their assumptions about the market as quickly as possible and adapt accordingly. The goal is to discover and launch a 'minimum viable product' that a group of customers are willing to buy before the startup exhausts its seed funding. This period is often referred to as the 'runway,' using the metaphor that a plane must build up enough momentum to take off before it crashes off the end of the tarmac. Fast, low-cost testing enables the runway to be extended.

Of course, some people choose to dive in, launch the business, and learn on the job. This clearly creates more stress in the startup process, but some say it sharpens their focus. There are several examples of commanders burning ships or bridges so that their armies could not retreat, leaving win or die as the only options. In the same way, launching your business provides a powerful incentive to exert your maximum effort to succeed. It is interesting that investors on shows like Shark Tank often expect entrepreneurs to be working full time on the business as a display of commitment. This shows they recognize the powerful motivational effects of making the business the founder's sole focus.

Another way to accelerate learning is to learn from others. In my experience, seasoned entrepreneurs greatly enjoy providing advice to new founders. For instance, the Small Business Administration (SBA) has a relationship with the Service Corps of Retired Executives (SCORE). SCORE provides free advice to small businesses across the United States. Similarly, the SBA maintains a network of Small

Business Development Centers (SBDCs) across the nation, which are focused on providing advice to startups and small businesses. Of course, thousands of entrepreneurship classes are also offered around the world that aim to teach aspiring entrepreneurs how to start a business. Books (like this one) can also be useful in pointing you in the right direction.

Putting together a 'board of advisors' is also a good way to solicit advice from a trusted group. Offering experienced executives a small piece of equity for some monthly (or ad hoc) advice can often accelerate the formation of a venture. Others see a benefit in joining peer groups like the Young President's Organization (YPO) or Entrepreneur Organization (EO). These groups bring together a cohort of CEOs from unrelated industries to discuss common problems, consider solutions, and provide support.

These choices may appear overwhelming at first, but the good news is there are plenty of ways for entrepreneurs to learn about starting a business. The biggest issue is often determining who is offering the most credible advice. My suggestion, for what it is worth, is to listen to those with the most experience and the greatest stake in being accurate. A board of advisors with equity in your firm has an incentive to give the best advice possible. A government employee at the SBDC with no skin in the game has much less incentive. On the other hand, an SBDC employee sees hundreds of firms each year and thus has a lot of experience with common problems and pitfalls. They also have the resources of the SBA and other SBDCs to support them. This experience, however, tends to be general knowledge that applies to a lot of small businesses. Experienced entrepreneurs in your industry will probably have valuable insights that go beyond the generic advice found in books and courses.

Ultimately, you will have to make a judgment about whose opinion to trust (including your own). Entrepreneurs are notorious for being over-confident, so developing sound judgment will be an on-going journey that never ends (but hopefully improves over time). The secret is to consult widely, take every opinion with a grain of salt, and test your assumptions whenever you can.

Ed is an entrepreneur

I first met Ed Hall in March 2017 when I was asked to speak about new venture financing to a group of budding entrepreneurs in Wilmington, North Carolina. Ed had an interesting back story. A Navy veteran, he completed a degree in entrepreneurship and film studies at UNC Wilmington in 2014. After graduation, he went on to manage Elite Innovations, a maker space that assisted entrepreneurs in new product development and prototyping, While there, he was involved in bringing 30 products to market.

Eager to fulfill a long-standing dream to start his own company, Ed became focused on the new technology emerging around the internet of things (or IoT). The internet of things refers to everyday devices that can interact with their users via modern communication networks and software. A Nest thermostat, which allows you to control the heating and air conditioning in your home, is a classic example of an IoT device. Growing up in a household with four pets, Ed saw the opportunity to create a family of IoT devices for pet care.

Like many new entrepreneurs, Ed started working on the idea part-time while still at Elite Innovations. However, by the end of 2015, Ed had secured seed funding from a local angel investor and was able to devote 100% of his efforts to Petrics, a company focused on pet wellness technology. Initially focused on a food dispenser, the company was forced to pivot when similar devices flooded the market from China. In 2017, he was able to secure a patent for pet health monitoring and analysis.[28] In January 2018, Petrics took the Consumer Electronics

Show by storm, with their connected pet bed being named a top 10 pick of the show by the Wall Street Journal.[29] Unfortunately, the product was not ready for manufacture and they had to turn down a lot of potential orders. Ed now estimates that the pet bed and associated software will hit the market later in 2020.

Ed is an embryonic entrepreneur because his company is still pre-revenue, but what struck me about my encounter with Ed was his unusual ability to listen. He politely asked about my opinion on his products and what I thought was the best way to 'monetize' his technology. It turns out that he asked the same question to everyone he met in the startup community. I asked him where this attitude came from. He replied, "I'm not arrogant enough to think that I can do something with absolutely no experience better than somebody else who has done it repeatedly. I ask...has anybody else found the solution?"

But he is also cautious to avoid what he calls 'mentor whiplash.' "You ask 10 people, you get 11 different opinions. You have to take some advice with a grain of salt. You really have to weigh the credibility of the individuals," he said. He goes on to observe that, "I had so many people coming to me and giving me advice and some of them did not know what they were talking about...some just wanted to put themselves on a pedestal." He feels that new entrepreneurs also need to be wary of successful entrepreneurs. "I need to be careful not to change my business model because this person that's done well has an entirely different business and different markets," he said. He found that those who gave the best feedback were the most reluctant to give advice, asked a lot of questions, and really tried to understand the business. They also tended to have the most experience in business.

Ed has a strong team of mentors and advisors, including veterinarians and others in the pet industry. He even tried reaching out to Jim Doherty, the CEO of PetSmart, who referred him to some other contacts. "People shouldn't be scared to reach out to these people...you'd be surprised, some of them actually do respond." Working in the maker space was also a great place to discover new technology, meet people in the startup community, and spark ideas. His degree in entrepreneurship also taught him some important skills and introduced him to people in the community. Time will tell whether Petrics will succeed in the market but Ed continues to do a lot of things right in his approach to learning from others.

Summary

It should be clear from the preceding discussion that an embryonic entrepreneur has a lot of work to do to bring a product to market. These activities might include perfecting a technology, finding manufacturers and distributors, marketing to customers, and hiring employees.

In some cases, these activities can be done very quickly with little initial outlay before the first dollar is earned. In other cases, like Cannamix and Petrics, there is a long lead time before products hit the market. Entrepreneurs are well-advised to find solutions that already exist to many of these problems and 'not reinvent the wheel.'

Entrepreneurs may be reluctant to ask others for advice, but the problem is often too much advice, rather than too little. An entrepreneur must therefore also develop some critical faculties to distinguish fact from fiction. However, even with good intentions, advice can be flawed as it might not translate to the specific context of your startup.

Emerging Entrepreneurs

Soon after graduating from the University of Tennessee in 1990, Dave Rose joined ADP selling payroll, human resources, automated time & attendance software and services. Rising rapidly through the ranks, he was promoted to Director of Sales in 1998. He then branched out into running sales, marketing, and business development for a number of startups, before founding and operating Kudzu Media Group from 2007-2010 and serving as Chief Operations Officer for MagnetVideo from 2010-2013. During his time at MagnetVideo he also completed an MBA at UNC Chapel Hill.

In 2013, Dave met Chuck Rinker. Chuck was an accomplished computer graphics engineer with a history of work with the US military, NASA, and EA Sports. Chuck had been working on a new technology to project three-dimensional holographic images onto portable screens to create life size, intelligent, digital assistants. The holograms were designed to assist and in some cases replace humans who might spend much of their time distributing information to visitors or customers. Applications included virtual receptionists, trade show booth ambassadors, and virtual concierges. The virtual assistants could be given any likeness and programmed to communicate in any language. Scripts could be uploaded via cellular networks and the customer or client could trigger different scripts (such as asking directions or requesting product information) via an iPad interface.

The touchscreen could also collect information from customers. The design used motion capture from real human actors reading each script so that the hologram's lip movements were as realistic as possible. The result was digital human capable of distributing timely information in an engaging fashion for a reasonably affordable price (particularly when factoring in the cost of a human attendant).

Chuck and Dave agreed to form a new company, PRSONAS, to pursue the development and deployment of the new technology, with Dave as Chief Executive Officer and Chuck as Chief Technology Officer. By 2016, PRSONAS had started to generate some sales traction, booking $700,000 in cumulative revenue from leading organizations such as the US Army, Microsoft, Expedia, and Procter & Gamble. There were also discussions with Ricoh, the copier company, to distribute their virtual assistants through the Ricoh sales organization. Dave used this opportunity to start raising seed funding to take PRSONAS to the next level of development.

By the end of 2017, PRSONAS had raised over $1 million, including $100,000 from AOL founder Steve Case. The company also won a Silicon Valley Open Doors pitch competition, and presented at Google's Demo Day. The firm also signed a distribution deal with Ricoh, anticipating $5 million in sales in the first year, and closing deals with Ricoh customers like Staples, Capital One, and Lennar. Cumulative revenue hit $1.5 million by the end of 2017. At the behest of Microsoft, PRSONAS also developed and patented the use of American Sign Language on their device.

However, in 2018, PRSONAS found itself unable to raise additional funds, forcing it to license its intellectual property back to Chuck's company, nuMedia Innovations. The firm was eventually acquired by nuMedia in October 2019. What went wrong? According to Dave, they were unable to attract investors to continue the development of the product and the market. They had run out of runway.

Advantages

An emerging enterprise is in a much stronger position than an embryonic startup. They are post-revenue but pre-profit, meaning they can partly fund their expenses through revenue. This usually means that the company has developed a minimum viable product and located an initial group of customers who are willing to pay for it.

However, almost by definition, an emerging enterprise is a temporary organization. Without a way to generate enough revenue to cover expenses, an organization will eventually fail. The good news is that the average profitable company hits this milestone after two years in business, and a small number of companies are profitable from day one. Other companies, like Amazon and Uber, have been able to extend their runway by raising new rounds of funding. In Amazon's case they were able to go for ten years before reporting a profit. However, the expectation is always there that a company will eventually become profitable.

Challenges

The PRSONAS case is not unusual. According to the Panel Study of Entrepreneurial Dynamics (PSED), about 75% of startups report some sort of initial revenue, but only 40% reach profitability within six years.[30] Furthermore, of those firms that reached initial profitability, about a third had disengaged from the business by the end of the study. This means that if we just focus on the startups that generate sales, about two in five will eventually make a profit, and one in four a sustained profit. Firms that raise funds from outside investors have about the same rate of success.

It is easy for a company to become distracted during this phase. Sometimes founders are in love with the technology and spend more time developing the next generation products rather than focusing on selling what works today. Another problem is the allure of venture capital (VC) funding. As we will see in the gazelle chapter, VCs want to back winners that can grow into billion-dollar companies that dominate their markets. Wanting to dominate a $100 million market is not enough for them. They want you to swing for the fences if you want their funding. This can tempt a company to change a successful smaller strategy to a more ambitious (and more expensive) goal. This may have happened to PRSONAS in 2017-18 when, partly at the behest of Google and Microsoft, they switched from selling holographic hardware to developing holographic software for any device.

Sustained profits are clearly the lifeblood of a business but calculating whether you are covering your expenses can be tricky. I once worked for an airline and the business model was quite straightforward. Lease or buy some planes, hire some pilots, and start selling seats for flights between cities. An airline can be cash flow positive in the short term if it covers the costs of marketing and flight operations via ticket sales. In the longer term, however, it also must invest in branding, maintenance, new aircraft, and pilot training. If the airline borrows money from investors to fund its startup and expansion, then it also has to factor in the cost of financing. Neglecting these longer-term issues will inevitably cause the downfall of the company even if it appears healthy in the short term. Depreciation is a non-cash charge that accountants subtract from revenue to account for the fact that assets will need to be repaired or replaced. Provisions are also made for taxes that must be paid. In theory, companies should be setting cash aside for these future expenses but sometimes owners forget they must cover these items.

Finally, there is the concept of opportunity cost. A self-employed plumber might take home $40,000 after expenses but could have made $60,000 working for someone else. A cash profit occurs when day-today revenues cover day-to-day expenses. An accounting profit occurs when revenue covers all accounting expenses, including provisions for future expenses like depreciation and taxes. An economic profit occurs when revenue also covers opportunity costs, which are the returns from the next best alternative to what you are doing. So technically, the plumber should deduct the $60,000 from accounting profit to determine economic profit. If that number is greater than zero then self-employment is a good choice, otherwise the plumber should get a job with someone else. Of course, the benefit of other factors like autonomy would have to be factored into any decision. Owners should also cover the opportunity cost of investor funds as they will move their funds (or refuse to invest more money) if they have better uses for their financial capital.

Ways to develop

What is the quickest path to profitability? Mathematically, the answer is simple. You can increase revenue or decrease expenses. Revenue, in turn, increases by bringing in more customers or increasing the amount spent per customer. These basic insights open a host of possible strategies. On the demand side, some companies turn to crowd funding, where they attempt to pre-sell their product to a group of backers before launch, thus ensuring they have funds to manufacture the product.

Bootstrapping is also a common strategy, where founders minimize expenses by borrowing or sharing resources. Working from your home or garage instead of an office is a way to keep costs down. Some entrepreneurs find co-working spaces a way to minimize the costs of establishing a physical location, while also benefiting from a downtown address and the ability to network with others in the startup community. In a co-working space, members only pay for the space they need, often sharing desks or meeting rooms with other members.

In more general terms, Steve Blank encourages founders to think of a startup as "a temporary organization designed to search for a repeatable and scalable business model."[31] A business model is a high-level understanding of how a business will make money. A business model is like a slot machine where you put a quarter in the top, pull the handle, and watch a dollar come out the bottom. A repeatable model transforms a quarter into a dollar every time the handle is pulled. A scalable model means you can build more machines that do the same thing.

A slot machine, however, is a black box. We do not exactly know how the quarter gets changed into a dollar. With a business model, however, you need to have an idea about how this transformation occurs. A business model, then, is a story about how you will change a quarter into a dollar, or for the more alchemically minded, turn lead into gold. For many years, founders were required to tell this story in the form of a business plan —a 20+ page document that laid out all the details on how a business was going to operate. Unfortunately, many founders spent more time writing a business plan than running their business! Today, entrepreneurs are encouraged to complete a one-page business model canvas that outlines how their business will work.[32] My preferred canvas, the Lean Canvas,[33] provides nine boxes for entrepreneurs to complete:

- Problem - what are your customer's top three problems?
- Solution - what is your solution to these problem(s)?
- Customer segments - who are your target customers?
- Channels - how will you reach your target customers?
- Unique value proposition - what is the single compelling message that turns a visitor into an interested prospect?
- Unfair advantage - what advantage do you have that can't be bought

or copied by others?

- Revenues - how much will you charge each customer?
- Costs - what are your costs to attract and serve a customer?

By answering these prompts, a founder (and investor) can get a good sense of how their sales volume, revenue, and costs might grow over time into a profitable business. In the case of PRSONAS, the problem was organizations that relied on expensive humans to disseminate basic information. The solution was to replace human workers with lifelike holograms. Initially, the company targeted receptionists and trade show attendants. The partnership with Ricoh enabled them to use Ricoh's existing sales organization to distribute their product. The unique value proposition was a little fuzzy. The holographs were cheaper than humans but more expensive than a digital touchscreen. The unfair advantage was the patented technology behind the holographic display that prevented competitors from copying their approach. Customers were charged a flat fee for the device plus an ongoing charge to upload content. The company had a good handle on their costs.

However, as Blank reminds us, creating a business model is only the start of the search for a sustainable business, something he calls 'customer discovery.' In most cases, the answers on the canvas are just assumptions or educated guesses. He advocates 'getting out of the building' and testing the most critical assumptions in the model to verify their accuracy. Only when all the assumptions have been thoroughly tested and verified should an organization start to invest heavily to scale their model. If an assumption cannot be verified, he recommends pivoting to another solution.

This approach is not suitable for all organizations. Steve Jobs was notoriously skeptical of market research, believing that customers did not always know what they wanted. Similarly, customers who say they like a product may also change their mind when asked to pay for it. Therefore, advocates of lean startup methodology advocate building a minimum viable product that some group of customers will buy to demonstrate that the product can meet a real need. Of course, just because a small group buys a product does not mean that a larger market exists or can be profitably accessed. But it is a start. Once a company is cash flow positive it has more breathing room to explore growth options.

It is also easier (i.e. cheaper) to pivot in the software industry. A founder can quickly alter code to add features or change a user interface. Other startups have less flexibility. Shirley, who we met in the previous chapter, has a patent for using hemp flour as an insecticide based on years of research, so there is limited flexibility to change the solution. PRSONAS also had a large investment in holographic technology. However, there is still work that can be done to find a specific way to deliver that solution to a given target segment. In these cases, prototypes can be useful as well as conducting product trials before entering full production.

Nick is an entrepreneur

Nick moved from South America to Las Vegas to make his fortune in the mid-2000s. In 2008, shortly after finishing his MBA in entrepreneurship, he started his first business. The business focused on teaching financial literacy to high school students and the timing was perfect. Las Vegas was in the throes of the global financial crisis and the state legislature had just passed a law that high schools should add financial literacy to their curriculum.

However, finding a sustainable business model proved elusive. Although high schools were required by law to teach the course, they had not been provided with any funds to acquire course materials.

Nick did everything he could to promote the business on a shoestring budget. He partnered with a teacher to write a curriculum, co-authored a book on financial literacy for young people, encouraged fellow MBA students to give guest lectures to school groups, visited schools, wrote directly to teachers, and gave free seminars to student clubs. Even after so much effort, the business was just not getting enough traction to make it profitable.

Shortly thereafter, Nick's father asked him to help sell a consignment of fruit in the United States from his farm. He had been shipping containers to the US for several years and was not happy with the prices he had been getting from his agents. Disillusioned with the education business, Nick moved to Los Angeles and tried to sell the fruit to local supermarkets. It was a tough sell. The fruit was still on the ship so he did not have samples to show the buyers. He admits that he probably made some terrible deals early on. He also realized that most fresh produce was bought from the LA wholesale market, which operated six days a week from 2 a.m. to noon.

One section of the wholesale market was heavily dominated by small immigrant traders, who sold fresh produce by the box to supermarkets and restaurants. Nick reasoned that his MBA and native Spanish would help him dominate this trade. He soon found a partner from Mexico and opened his own booth at the market. Within two years, he was bankrupt. It was a cut-throat business and contracts from buyers and sellers had a way of not being honored. Chastened, he moved back to Vegas in 2012 and left what remained of the business to his partner.

The only saving grace was a contact from Singapore who called him a few months later about finding some avocados. He had a good source for avocados and he was able to buy them on credit and ship them successfully to Singapore. Happy with the quality and service, the Singapore buyer called again looking for strawberries. Little by little, Nick started using the trusted connections he found in the Los Angeles market to start building a global supply chain network.

Even as late as 2015 he was not sure if the business would succeed. There just seemed to be so much to learn about global trading. He was constantly hustling to find the best produce on the best terms for his growing cadre of buyers. He found he was calling all over the world to get the best deals. One setback he faced was an error in his pricing spreadsheet that meant he was losing money on many of his deals. He even recalls calling his old employer about getting his casino job back.

But the company continued to grow and Nick continued to learn. He was profitable within one year. By 2020, he was operating in 65 countries, with an annual revenue approaching $100 million. "We work on small margins, but a small margin on 100 million is still a decent amount of money," he said. His goal is to grow into one of the largest produce traders in the world within a decade.

He admits that one of the key barriers to success is mental. "A lot of entrepreneurship is being able to put up with your own thoughts about how you are not going to make it," he said. He found self-help groups, like the Young Presidents' Organization (YPO), useful for dealing with the mental challenge. "I realized that I'm not alone in my struggle and everyone faces the same obstacles," he said. "Surrounding myself with people that are more successful has really inspired me and kept me aiming higher."

In hindsight, he claims that ignorance is bliss. If he'd known how hard he would have to work and how much money he would lose, he would have given up. But he also sees failure as an inevitable part of entrepreneurship. "Everybody that I know that's successful has had a failure at some point or multiple failures," he reflected. He credits the desperation that follows failure as one of his strongest motivators. He is also humbler about what it takes to succeed.

Summary

Emerging entrepreneurs are in the twilight zone between making their first dollar and turning a profit. As we saw, moving from revenue to profit is a difficult feat for most startups with only a third successfully making the transition. Entrepreneurs are therefore making a bet that their initial business model has all the right elements to succeed.

The reality, however, is that a lot of the assumptions in the model will be wrong. In fact, it's probably better to assume that *all* the assumptions in the model are wrong and approach the business like a jigsaw puzzle, asking, "How can I fit these pieces together to generate a return for myself?" In the cases above, both Dave and Nick discovered flaws in their initial business model.

Funds are limited, so a startup only gets a relatively short amount of time to experiment before running out of cash. Nick was able to pivot away from several ideas before finding a viable path to profitability. PRSONAS, on the other hand, tried several pivots but was unable to find its way to a profitable future. This doesn't mean that one founder worked harder or smarter than the other. However, I do think it's important for founders to keep their eye on the ball. After generating revenue, profitability should be the most important milestone for every startup. Spending time laying the groundwork for some giant future business is usually not advisable unless that foundation is established first. The exception, as we have seen, is if you are seeking to quickly dominate an emerging market. We will examine these types of situations in more detail in the chapter on high-growth firms.

Finally, unlike a game, business is not something you win. A business model must be constantly adjusted in light of changing economic conditions, regulations, competition, and technology. It is not a 'one-and-done' situation. Successful entrepreneurs are constantly tweaking their business model to seize new opportunities and counter threats.

This is the best way to ensure your continued success well into the future.

III

The Lifestyle Entrepreneur

The desire for autonomy, not profit, is the number one reason that people give for entering into self-employment. In other words, they desire to be independent and personally direct how they work and live. This often means substituting self employment for paid employment, earning about the same either way. It can also mean taking a side gig and working part time to make a little extra cash for the family.

Craft Entrepreneurs

Fortunato, or Lucky, as he was called in English, arrived in Australia from Sicily with his wife and three children in 1960, part of the massive post-war immigration program initiated by the Australian government. The oldest of seven siblings, he was the last to emigrate to Australia, arriving with just a pair of suitcases and the clothes on his back.

A house painter by trade, and an artist by vocation, he worked for the next forty years painting and flipping houses. He also produced fine art landscapes of Italian and Australian vistas in his garage, painted in oils on canvas, and then enclosed them in elaborate frames. He sold these paintings to other members of the Italian community, always through word of mouth, with people showing up in the early evenings to look at paintings and drink a little *espresso*.

Lucky was also an entrepreneur. Apart from the odd apprentice, he did not employ anyone, but he was self-employed all his life. Like most people in trade, he minimized his risk by collecting cash for materials before starting a job. But he risked his labor, collecting cash for his work at the end of a job, betting that the client would be satisfied with his work. Invariably, his clients were happy, and he enjoyed a steady cash flow. The fact that most of his work came through word-of-mouth from the Italian community no doubt contributed to his high collection rate.

Lucky took more risks with house flipping, putting 20% down, borrowing the remainder, contributing time and materials, and then selling the finished product. But he also had several advantages in this business. His extended Italian family had members from every trade - electricians, plumbers, carpenters - people he could always trust to show up and do a good job at short notice. As a result, he successfully flipped several apartments and houses over the years.

Lucky's story is not unusual. Around 15 million workers or 10% of the total workforce in the United States describe themselves as primarily self-employed.[34] About 6 in 10 of these workers are unincorporated, meaning they do not officially own a company. Unincorporated workers are more than twice as likely to work in the construction or extraction industries. Furthermore, only 14% of the unincorporated group have paid employees, compared with 42% of their counterparts in the incorporated group. Foreign-born workers are also more likely to be self-employed than native-born workers. Immigrants are often attracted to self-employment, either because they lack formal education or because their qualifications are not recognized in their new country.

A craft entrepreneur, then, is an individual who works full-time or part-time in a trade, technical, arts, craft, or hobby business that is often unincorporated. The defining characteristic of a craft entrepreneur is individual talent, that is, being good at something. This talent may have been innate or acquired over time through a hobby or apprenticeship. Often, it is a combination of nature and nurture with 10,000 hours of dedicated practice required to become an expert in anything according to Malcolm Gladwell.[35] The term therefore encompasses millions of people, including those who consume their own product and sell the surplus (think home brewers), the building trades, artists, and musicians.

Historically, the term craft entrepreneur has had a mixed reputation.

Initially associated with the craft guilds of the middle ages, the craftsman started as an apprentice, progressed to journeyman, and finally achieved the title of master, after completing a 'masterpiece.' Master craftsmen were highly respected in their community but had strict standards about prices, hours of operation, product quality, and competition. After the rise of industrialization and the decline of the guilds, it became associated with blue collar workers and 'mom and pop' operations. The term craft entrepreneur was first used by N.R. Smith in 1967, who defined it as someone "having a narrowness in education and training, low social awareness and involvement, a feeling of incompetence in dealing with the social environment, and a limited time orientation."[36] Opportunistic entrepreneurs, on the hand, were growth-oriented, adaptive, and highly educated. Craft entrepreneurs were more focused on making a good living than maximizing profits and were therefore considered inferior to the 'true' opportunistic entrepreneurs.

More recently, Blake Mathias in *Wearing Many Hats* has argued that craft entrepreneurs "do not make decisions in order to optimize venture growth but instead to heighten (or maintain) the quality of their product. Put differently, they refuse to take actions that might help their firm grow, if it means sacrificing who they are and what they do."[37] In this view, being a craft entrepreneur is more about identity than financial gain. Authenticity seems to play a big role and, as we have seen, autonomy is also a factor in why people choose self-employment. Paradoxically, this emphasis on quality and authenticity can sometimes lead to growth as consumers reject mass market brands that are focused on quantity over quality.

Advantages

Craft entrepreneurs are often doing what they know and what they love. Lucky loved to paint. When he wasn't painting a house, he was down in his garage putting oils on canvas. As the old saying goes, "When you do what you love, you don't work a day in your life." Not surprisingly, self-employed workers have the highest level of job satisfaction of any occupational group.

A focus on quality also ensures a steady demand for your work as your reputation grows. In good times, a craft entrepreneur can make a good living without taking on employees or opening multiple locations. Craft entrepreneurs also have the luxury of choosing their own hours and vacations. These businesses are also ideal as a side hustle for households seeking extra income, including stay-at-home parents raising children, because the hours can be adjusted around other paid or unpaid work.

Another big advantage of self-employment is the low barriers to entry. A recent survey found that one third of small businesses got started with less than $5,000.[38] Funds are typically sourced from personal finances such as savings, a credit card or home equity line of credit. Educational requirements are often low for this work as well. There is no degree required to open a cleaning business, a cafe, or craft brewery for instance.

Challenges

In bad times, it can be tough to find customers as a self-employed person. Self-employed and gig workers were among the hardest hit in the recent COVID-19 pandemic for instance. In developing countries, workers are often driven by necessity rather than opportunity. Growing vegetables and selling them at the local market might be the only form of income available to them. In developed countries, the ranks of the self-employed have been falling for decades now as large retail chains have displaced mom and pop operations, and the lack of benefits and rising student debt make it more difficult for workers to subsist without a steady paycheck from an employer. On the other hand, gig work and side hustles have proliferated as workers seek to supplement their income or undertake more fulfilling roles beyond their main income source.

Similarly, while the promise of flexible hours is appealing, there is no free lunch. Research shows that self-employed workers tend to work longer hours and get paid less than employed counterparts with similar qualifications. In some ways, this the cost of autonomy. Self-employed workers are willing to sacrifice some income and benefits for the joy of not answering to a boss. This does not mean that everyone craves the same autonomy. For some, following orders is not a big deal. For those who do have a hard time in such an environment it might be the right choice to seek self-employment. In fact, some entrepreneurs might even find it difficult to hold down a regular job.

Another challenge facing craft entrepreneurs is the rise in licensing and regulation. The number of Federal regulations almost doubled in the forty years from 1976 to 2016.[39] Licensing can act as a barrier to entry for craft entrepreneurs, who must undertake training and testing to be admitted to a field. For example, according to the Council of Economic Advisors, California's Board of Barbering and Cosmetology required 1600 hours of education and hands-on training to take a licensing test for cosmetology.[40] In addition to the direct costs of the training, there are also other hidden costs, including: the hours of lost income that could have been earned while training, the compliance costs of demonstrating you are licensed and certified, the costs of fines and other legal action for violating the rules, and the costs of staying abreast of changes in the rules. All of these actions create challenges for entrepreneurs and reduce the rate of new business formation.

Ways to develop

There are a number of ways to develop or 'level up' as a craft entrepreneur. The first way is to continue doing what you love and hone your skills to a higher level. There are always new techniques and materials, new ways of doing things, and a higher level of technical achievement that can be attained. The quality of your work, in turn, acts as an advertisement for your business and has the potential to attract new customers.

One of the down sides of a craft business is the level of competition. While the low barriers to entry mean it is easy for an individual entrepreneur to start a craft business, this ease of entry also attracts many competitors into the field. A second recommendation is to find a niche for your talents that shields you as much as possible from this competition. As an Italian immigrant, Lucky was able to focus on the needs of fellow Italian immigrants, a sizable part of the Melbourne population, but also difficult for native Australians to access due to language and cultural barriers. This niche allowed Lucky to draw on referrals from family and friends, and ensure there was sufficient demand for his skills for many years.

Another way to become more competitive is to learn to hustle. The real estate business is a notoriously competitive market, with thousands of agents competing to represent buyers and sellers. Agents all have access to the same information via the local multiple listing service (MLS), and all use personal vehicles, cell phones, and email to conduct business. Nevertheless, a small proportion of agents dramatically outperform other agents, often by an order of magnitude. It turns out that these successful agents do things that other agents do not (or will not) do. They execute better and they are more alert to fleeting opportunities.

Better execution means they make fewer mistakes with their transactions. Contracts are completed correctly, supporting services (like title agents and banks) are coordinated better, and there is a high level of communication. This is not just being better skilled at the immediate tasks of being a realtor but also choreographing all other moving parts that make the experience as a whole a pleasant one for the client.

Successful agents are also better at anticipating customer needs. When they learn that a client has a new job, they contact him or her immediately about listing the house. When they receive a new listing, they contact former clients to see if there is any interest. Not randomly or mechanically but in a targeted, judicious way. If a given client is not interested, they follow up to see if they know someone else who might be interested. They find a thousand ways to stay in touch, including sending newsletters and holiday messages. They are also alert to problems, and work on resolving issues as quickly as possible.

Another simple hack is to engage in some low-cost marketing. Even in 2018, around 40% of small businesses did not have a website.[41] Creating one, and keeping it up to date, can be a way to differentiate yourself from others. Similarly, having the discipline to regularly post on social media is a way to create your 'personal brand.' Even setting up your business as a location on Google Maps can drive business when people seek to find a business like yours nearby.

Finally, given the inevitable increase in the number of rules and regulations, it makes sense for a craft entrepreneur to find a good accountant, insurance agent, and lawyer. Although often viewed as expensive, these professionals can be worth their weight in gold if they help you avoid (or minimize) complicated tax or compliance issues. Often, talking to other small business owners or the local chamber of commerce can be a good way to find some competent professionals at a reasonable price.

Peter is an entrepreneur

My father, Peter, was born in Frankston, a small township on Port Philip Bay, about 30 miles southeast of Melbourne, two weeks before the outbreak of the Second World War. His father was a gardener and later a farm manager. His mother was a nurse. His parents met at a sanatorium where my grandmother was nursing tuberculosis patients.

Peter worked for a branch of the federal government for 40 years. When he started it was known as the Post Master General's department (or the PMG), then Telecom Australia, and now Telstra. He laid telephone wires for a living, traveling around the state to provide plain old telephone service to rural Australians. Later, he became an instructor, teaching others his craft.

Peter was also an entrepreneur. For five years in the late 1970s and early 1980s, he had a side hustle renting a fleet of caravans (or travel trailers as they are known in the US) to families in my small hometown of 70,000 people. Starting with four caravans, or vans, as trailers are known in Australia, our backyard ended up hosting eight vans on a quarter-acre lot. I have memories of my father moving vans around as rentals went out and came in. Heaving and hauling on the jockey wheel at the front of the trailer, he maneuvered them up and down the narrow drive, and around the yard, all times of the day and night. My stay-at-home mother also pitched in, helping to clean the vans when they returned.

One day, the vans disappeared. In their place, my father built an extension to our three-bedroom house, adding an extra bedroom, a bonus room, and a bathroom so my two brothers and I had our own rooms. He always said the profits from the caravan business paid for the extension on the house.

He and my mother went on to another side hustle working with Dominant, an Amway-style multi-level marketing business, based in Australia. They proceeded to recruit a small downline and buy the products themselves. Even now, forty years later, they still use Dominant products. My parents sold their four-bedroom family home after their sons left school, and bought a modest, newly constructed, three-bedroom house one street away from the original house.

My father was no Steve Jobs or Elon Musk. He did not invent anything, he did not raise money from investors, he had no employees, and he did not grow his business into a multi-billion dollar corporation. His net worth cannot be measured in the millions or billions of dollars. Some people would dispute whether he was a 'real' entrepreneur, probably because he never gave up his secure day job. He was never fully self-employed.

And yet, he showed several other characteristics of an entrepreneur. He saw an opportunity and he raised capital to pursue that opportunity. He borrowed money to buy equipment, and risked his own modest down payment in the process. He also promoted the business, kept the books, and managed the operations of renting and recovering his assets.

In the Dominant business, like most multi-level marketing concerns, my parents' primary job was to grow a downline and earn a small commission from downline sales. They invested virtually none of their own financial capital but, as a partnership, they were able to write off the expenses of growing their little enterprise. More importantly, they invested their human capital and social capital in the enterprise. My father was a wage earner all his life and wouldn't show up in ranks of the self-employed. Nevertheless, he was a part-time entrepreneur for much of his life.

Summary

Craft entrepreneurs are the most common type of entrepreneur. They prefer to work for themselves and they have a skill that is valued by the market. Often, they are passionate about the products they create.

Historically, being a craftsman, particularly a master craftsman, was a significant achievement but the industrial revolution meant that machines soon overtook humans in a range of traditional industries. As a result, craft entrepreneurs came to be seen as backwards and perhaps not even 'true' entrepreneurs. I think this is wrong. Up to 27% of the workforce is earning some sort of self-employment income.[42] They are all risking their time and (limited) treasure for a better life and deserve a little respect.

That being said, this is a very competitive space, as the barriers to entry are often low. The ability to hustle to provide superior service and find a niche are two important keys to success. The resurgence of craft industries, like brewing and handmade items, is also a signal that consumers are beginning to appreciate the authenticity and personality of individual pieces, further expanding opportunities in this area.

Virtual Entrepreneurs

H unter Hastings was born to a working-class family in England shortly after the end of the Second World War. At that time, class was destiny. Without the right pedigree, an English worker was almost always denied access to the 'inner ring' of career opportunities in both the public and private sectors.

Hunter's big break came in 1966 with a scholarship to Jesus College at Cambridge University. The Cambridge pedigree opened doors and he was able to secure a position with consumer giant Procter & Gamble soon after graduation. In 1986, he took a position as Vice President at a startup called Ryan Partnership, which had launched in 1984 as a packaged goods consultancy and rapidly grew into a fully fledged consumer marketing agency. In 1999, In 1999, he was approached to become CEO of a marketing technology company called Emmperative, owned by Procter & Gamble, which aimed to commercialize project management software for product managers. However, the dotcom crash scuttled the company's prospects, and he then turned his hand to consultancy, owning and operating his own marketing firm for the past 20 years.

Hunter sees the internet age as a boon for virtual entrepreneurs, stating, "There are new ways to assemble resources whether it's labor or capital or anything else. These days you can assemble it over the internet you can get your manufacturing done in China and your retail done on Amazon." Hunter recently wrote a book about this new age, titled *The Interconnected Individual: Seizing Opportunity in the Era of AI, Platforms, Apps, and Global Exchanges.* According to Hunter, wondrous things are now possible. "A kid with an iPad can design a blouse, and software can disassemble it and say the buttons are going to be made in Bangladesh and the cotton is going to be sourced from India and then we'll assemble it in Pakistan and we'll ship them to be there next week," he said. The vast majority of entrepreneurs have no employees but Hunter sees this as a strength rather than a weakness, noting, "You would call that a zero employee business but actually it's a supply chain."

In the preface of his book, he comes full circle back to his working class origins. While teaching project-based learning at Hult International Business School, he discovered that pedigree issues were still creating bottlenecks at large companies. These companies continued to hire from the same elite universities and refused to provide projects for students from non-elite colleges. For Hunter, technology provides a way to bypass these constraints and democratize access to opportunity. As Milton Berle famously quipped, "If opportunity doesn't knock, build a door."

Technology is allowing entrepreneurs to build those new doors every day, mostly online. The virtual entrepreneur is most definitively a product of the internet age. The World Wide Web opened to the public in August 1991 but residential network speeds were very slow (around 0.03 megabits per second). Future internet giants Amazon and eBay were born in 1994 and 1995, respectively. Google arrived on the scene in 1998. The dotcom boom between 1995 and 2000 saw an explosion in websites and internet infrastructure. By 2002, residential internet speeds had passed 1 megabit per second, enabling websites to use more sophisticated graphics and multimedia. Today, residential internet speeds routinely exceed 100 megabits per second, with services up to 2,000 megabits per second (or 2 gigabits/sec) in some areas.[43]

At the same time, the rise of mobile devices, cellular networks and Wi-Fi have made the internet a mobile (and global) phenomenon. Cell phone companies are in the process of phasing out fourth generation (4G) networks, with maximum speeds of 100 megabits per second, in favor of 5G networks with maximum speeds of 10,000 megabits per second (i.e. 10 gigabits/second). The widespread availability of networks has allowed everyday devices (like thermostats and washing machines) to be connected and share data with their users, creating an 'Internet of Things.' Data is routinely being stored 'in the cloud' leading to a plethora of companies seeking to access, interpret, and react to patterns in this 'big data,' often with the help of sophisticated algorithms.

Advantages

A virtual entrepreneur can literally run a business from anyplace that has a screen connected to the web. For introverts, like me, this means working from home in front of a desktop computer or laptop. I can also work in front of a tablet or cell phone but the smaller screen sizes and limited keyboard options make them a bit unwieldy. For those with a more social bent, there are options for co-working in almost any city or town in the United States. Co-workers share amenities, including desks, meeting rooms, and office services, while working on independent projects. Higher end co-working spaces might also include recreational facilities, like a bar or pool table. We are also seeing the emergence of co-living spaces, where virtual workers can share living and working facilities with other virtual denizens (see outsite.co for some examples).

Arguably, there has never been an easier time to start a business. Government forms have migrated online and several sites specialize in providing packages to form a limited liability company in any state.

Banking and payment transactions have also been greatly improved in the internet age. Anyone with a cell phone can send and receive payments almost anywhere on the planet. It is also easier to promote your business, with Facebook and Google offering simple ways to reach targeted demographics on a pay-per-action basis (rather than the pay per view options of traditional media). Websites, like Alibaba, also make it easier to find suppliers in other countries, particularly China.

Once a product has been created, it can be sold on a variety of platforms, including eBay, Amazon, and Etsy. Global shipping companies also facilitate the flow of goods from producers to customers. In fact, an entrepreneur might never see or take physical possession of a product, because the capability exists to have items 'drop shipped' directly from a third-party warehouse to the customer. In the case of digital products, like electronic books or software, the need for physical delivery has ceased altogether.

In short, technology in the internet age has dramatically lowered the costs of coordinating value chains. A value chain is the set of steps a product must go through to reach the hands of a customer, from raw materials to production to warehouse to sales to delivery. In the past, a company might own all of the stages of production or use agents to coordinate transactions between stages. Today, however, those stages can be operated independently and the role of agents has greatly diminished, as end users can now communicate directly with operators as different stages of the value chain (a process known as disintermediation). Hunter uses the metaphor of a maestro to argue that a virtual entrepreneur is a master conductor that meshes a set of independent providers into a coherent whole, much like a conductor blends a group of disparate instruments into a pleasing performance.

Finally, the use of independent providers at each stage allows the virtual entrepreneur to scale easily and cheaply. Delivery giants like FedEx, UPS, and DHL have little problem handling the extra volume if your business doubles or triples in size overnight. Similarly, cloud providers like Amazon and Microsoft don't require large upfront payments to buy more servers if your business finds overnight success. They have pre-built capacity on demand.

Challenges

A virtual entrepreneur faces three major challenges: the level of competition, the fragility of the supply chain, and how to find and keep trusted partners. The largest challenge facing virtual entrepreneurs is the level of competition in the space. The barriers to start and operate a global business have not just fallen for one entrepreneur, they have fallen for *all* entrepreneurs. This can readily be seen on sites like Amazon or eBay, where dozens of suppliers compete in every product category. Competition is great for consumers, who can find lower prices, but tough for those trying to make a living.

Take books, for example. In 2013, almost 500,000 books were self-published with an international standard book number (or ISBN). By 2018, that number had grown to almost 1.7 million books per year![44] The average digital book sells about 250 copies in its lifetime, while a traditional publisher might sell around 3,000 copies on average. Neither route is going to make an author (or publisher) rich. In fact, online publishers now encourage authors to think of a book as a gateway to other revenue sources like speaking, consulting, or a lucrative dream job.

The reality is that climbing to the top of the heap is work! The 100 most notable books in 2014 had median sales of 25,000 copies[45]. Those nominated for prizes, like the Pulitzer Prize, reached 75,000 sales per year on average. Finding a way to stand out in the crowd has always been tough, but the crowd is now global and quick to imitate new ideas. Staying competitive is an ongoing challenge.

At the time of writing, the COVID-19 pandemic has greatly disrupted international supply chains, highlighting the fragility of our interconnected world. While many suppliers are available to serve a particular client, once a supplier is chosen then the entrepreneur is highly dependent on that supplier, due to the cost and delay of finding a new supplier. Any disruption to the supplier's operation will cause a ripple effect downstream that affects the distributor's ability to serve an end user. Suppliers, in turn, are dependent on those supplying the inputs to them, as well as the transport networks that distribute their products to the distributor and, ultimately, the consumer.

Sometimes, disruptions to the supply chain are unavoidable, such as the quarantining that occurred during the COVID-19 crisis. Other times, a disruption can occur because the supplier acts in a self-serving way. Also known as opportunism or holdup, the behavior hurts the virtual entrepreneur's business because the supplier fails to honor a commitment in some way. For instance, I once advised a company that sold custom furniture in the US, which was manufactured on demand in China. The company was experiencing complaints from customers about damaged furniture. Pieces were arriving with large scratches in their fine finishes despite the packaging being labeled as fragile and 'handle with care.' The problem was trying to find out where the damage was occurring. Was it:

- when the parts arrived at the factory,
- during the manufacturing process,
- when the finished furniture was loaded into the shipping container and driven to the docks,
- during the loading, transit, or unloading of the container ship,
- when the items were put in a warehouse in Los Angeles,
- when they were shipped by truck to the customer,
- during the assembly of the furniture by a third-party assembler, or

- all of the above?

A bad actor has an incentive to cut corners to increase his or her own profits. Long supply chains, like the one above, make it difficult to detect bad actors, which in turn makes it difficult to assign liability and receive compensation. The biggest challenge, however, is the threat to the startup's brand as poor customer experiences lead to poor reviews. Customers assume these supply chain problems have been solved (or at least minimized). Getting to that stage requires a lot of work, particularly when the various parts are not under your direct control.

Ways to develop

The only way to beat your competition is to be better in some way. Sometimes that means you work harder than anyone else, but it can also mean that you work smarter. Many virtual entrepreneurs have complained to me about the numerous problems involved in managing a complex supply chain. I remind them that they are literally getting paid to solve those problems. If it was easy then everyone would be doing it, and no one would be making money. All profit comes from scarcity, that is, doing something that is rare and difficult for others to pull off.

Angela Duckworth, a professor at Wharton, has written extensively about the concept of grit, which she defines as a combination of passion and perseverance.[46] Duckworth sees grit as a set of behaviors like focus, having a positive attitude, learning to persevere, and setting challenging goals. These behaviors, in turn, can be learned or developed. Duckworth's critics have pointed out that grit is highly correlated with the psychological trait of conscientiousness, a trait that is relatively constant over an individual's lifespan. If true, this means that gritty individuals are born, not made. My own take is that we all start at different positions on a continuum but that we can improve from any level. As a natural introvert, I might never become a gregarious extrovert, but I can become more extroverted over time.

This is important because research shows that 'stick-to-it-iveness' is a key factor in entrepreneurial success. Entrepreneurs that hustle every day for many years tend to be more successful than those who work in short bursts. For instance, a recent survey comparing successful authors (earning more than $100,000 a year) with emerging authors found some large differences.[47] Successful authors spent 46% more time writing per week than emerging authors (28 vs 20 hours). They had also been writing on average three years before finding success. As a result, they had published more books than emerging writers and were able to earn income from multiple revenue streams. Grit, then, is about seeing the business as a marathon rather than a sprint. It is particularly important for virtual entrepreneurs because of speed of change in online services.

The online world is constantly evolving and new tools are developed every day to solve the problems that virtual entrepreneurs encounter. Part of working smarter involves staying up to date with these developments. For instance, the furniture problem discussed earlier was solved by hiring a company that specialized in quality control. A Chinese-speaking American engineer saw an opportunity to hire a crew of Chinese engineers to inspect every stage of the process, providing reports and photos of items in transit. As a result, the source of the quality control problem was quickly identified and resolved. Startups that knew about this company were able to dramatically improve their customer experience, thus differentiating themselves from other competitors.

Leading companies are often first movers or fast followers of new technology. First movers can grab customers or valuable positions before others enter the market. Unfortunately, they also have to bear the costs of fixing buggy software and educating the market on new ways of doing things. Fast followers wait for the kinks to be worked out. then rapidly implement the best solution to stay ahead of most of their competitors. In both cases, the winners are at the front of the pack. An entrepreneur should always be tinkering with the business to find new and better ways to work faster and smarter. Examples abound of new software-as-a-service (SaaS) offerings that make life easier for virtual entrepreneurs, including payment systems, payroll services, accounting products, and hiring solutions.

The final piece of advice to virtual entrepreneurs is to find ways to solve the trust problem. In the furniture example, more monitoring was undertaken to ensure that damage was minimized. This does not work for every business. In some cases, monitoring the quality of an item can be prohibitively expensive or difficult to measure. The alternative to outsourcing quality control would have been to station a US inspector in China or have someone fly back and forth. In both cases, the ability of the inspector to examine every part of the supply chain would have been limited and a large drain on the resources of the startup.

One solution is to rely on online ratings. Suppliers can be rated by retailers just as customers can rate retailers. However, as we know, ratings often have to be taken with a grain of salt as fake reviews can be generated and reviewers can be paid. Amazon's use of 'verified reviewers' is an attempt to halt these practices. Other companies build a brand by offering trusted reviews. Strong brands, in general, are also a signal of reliability as companies have an incentive to perform well to preserve the value of the brand.

Another useful technique is to build up a level of trust and commitment over time. Start with small orders, then give more business to suppliers that continue to deliver on time and on budget with

73

the requisite level of quality. Sourcing from two suppliers can be complicated and cost a little more, but gives more insurance against a disruption in your supply chain. If one supplier has an issue, then some or all of your business can be moved to the other supplier. Your first solution might not work out but having the grit to continually experiment will hopefully improve your results over time.

Roli is a virtual entrepreneur

I first met Roli in the spring of 2004. An Israeli by birth, he had moved to the US in search of opportunities. By the time I met him, he had already established a successful business importing items from China and selling them on eBay. His strategy to minimize competition was to identify innovative products that appealed to a small segment of the US population. However, the niche had to be large enough to sell at least one shipping container of product. One example was selling an attachment to a popular brand of tractor that allowed farmers to dig holes for fence posts.

Roli operated his business as a one-man show. He traveled to China to select products, arranged for shipping and warehousing, posted items on eBay, and handled customer inquiries directly. As his confidence and experience grew, he began to import containers to other countries, eventually operating in Australia, North America, and Europe — all from the comfort of his own sofa.

One day Roli called me up and said he had a problem. He had been selling mini bikes in Europe but the authorities had determined that the CE mark for the bikes was fraudulent. A CE mark certifies that the equipment complies with European standards for health, safety, and environmental protection. Roli quickly determined that his Chinese suppliers had lied about having a valid mark. Unfortunately, distributing products without a CE mark was a serious offence in

Europe, punishable by asset seizure, major fines, and potentially even jail time!

Undeterred, Roli turned his full attention to solving the problem. For two days and two nights, he called suppliers, testing services, European customs officials, trade lawyers, and fellow importers trying to find a solution to his dilemma. Most of them told him there was nothing that could be done. Finally, he found a lawyer willing to negotiate with the right government officials. After some wrangling, the government agreed to drop the charges and release his merchandise if he could secure a CE mark within two weeks. This set off a flurry of calls to China, where he was able to arrange for an authorized testing service to visit his Chinese supplier and return the results to the regulator within the desired time frame. Not long after this incident, Roli made the determination that competition on eBay was becoming too intense, even for niche products, and started to pivot toward new opportunities.

I asked Roli about the keys to entrepreneurial success and whether those factors could be developed. He listed drive, problem-solving, risk-taking, networking, negotiation skills, persuasion, and listening as his key success factors. Of these, he felt that problem-solving and drive were the most difficult factors to develop. He also mentioned that he had displayed an ability to get others to cooperate with him from a young age. Interestingly, he felt that risk-taking and listening were skills that could be developed over time.

Summary

Hunter's case demonstrates that opportunities continue to emerge for virtual entrepreneurs to find a following and create a sustainable, potentially highly profitable, business online. In fact, it has never been easier to create a virtual organization. However, being a virtual entrepreneur also comes with a set of challenges. Competition is intense, and bad actors abound. Lengthy supply chains are also subject to disruption even when all parties have the best of intentions.

Virtual entrepreneurs can mitigate these factors in a number of ways. First, they need to be constantly learning about new technologies that can make their operations more efficient and provide their customers with a better experience. Being a fast follower of new trends in your industry seems like the best way to go.

Another strategy is to expect that problems will naturally arise. Complex supply chains will always have problems with coordination (making things mesh together) and cooperation (ensuring others act in your interests). Learning to solve those problems for yourself and others is often what makes a business successful. Solving these problems as they arise requires a good dose of grit. As Roli's case demonstrated, continuing to work on a problem and not taking "no" for answer can often get you out of the stickiest of situations.

IV

The Employer Entrepreneur

Taking on employees represents the next stage in complexity for a venture.
In doing so, entrepreneurs must learn to become managers of people.

Family Business Owners

D avid owns a quarter share in a family restaurant serving Mediterranean fare to residents in the north-eastern suburbs of Melbourne. His other partners are his younger brother, mother, and father. They opened their first restaurant together in 2000, in another location, about 5 miles further north. They have been at the present location since 2007.

David's case is interesting because he turned down a career in international taxation at one of the big four accounting firms. From a young age, he knew he wanted to be in business. He admits that he only attended an accounting information session because he heard that some girls would be there (which was a big deal for a 17-year-old boy at a boy's only school)! After five rounds of interviews, he was offered a place in the prestigious PriceWaterhouseCoopers traineeship program, which combined paid work with part-time study for an accounting degree. David initially enjoyed the social aspects of the program, but found public accounting to be boring, and came to dislike the water cooler gossip sessions every Monday morning. He resented being asked to cut his hair. But what he found the most irritating of all was getting billed out to high net worth clients at $65 per hour while only getting paid $15 per hour. "Wait on," he said, "I want to be the one getting paid $65 an hour."

So he was pleased (and a little anxious) when PwC failed to offer him a permanent position at the end of his program. During the summer, he had borrowed some money from a friend and worked with his grandfather to flip a house, making $30,000 in profit. His father then suggested, "Why don't we use the money to start a restaurant in the local strip mall?" And their first restaurant was born, with his father and brother working in the back, and his mother and sister working the front of the house. In addition to working both front and back of house, David also managed the financial aspects of the business.

The business was a local sensation. Good food, good prices, and good service generated repeat business and positive word of mouth, with some customers eating there multiple times a week. The restaurant business really exploded when they were discovered by the local university and became a favored lunchtime eating place for the president and other senior administrators.

Seven years later, David decided to open a second, larger location in an upscale part of town. The plan was to leave his parents to run the first location and use the second location to support a growing family. To cover the initial startup costs, he entered into a partnership with someone outside the family, borrowed money for an expensive fit-out, and hired one of the top chefs in town to create a stunning new menu. It did not work out. Shortly after their grand opening, the chef started to become unreliable, and it was eventually discovered that he had a substance abuse problem. The quality of the food declined and the negative reviews grew. Monthly revenues fell precipitously and the bank started calling about their payments.

David called his family for help. They fired all the kitchen staff, including the head chef, replacing them with family. At the same time they bought out the other partner, in the process being forced to sell their initial location. The gambit worked and the restaurant was nursed back to health, supporting an extended family of five, which has now grown to 11, over the last 12 years.

80

Advantages

The opening case illustrates some of the advantages of a family business. Trust and loyalty are both major factors. It is no coincidence that the most successful early banking systems were run by families. The Medici family bank was created in 1397 and operated in several locations throughout Europe. Mayer Rothschild created a pan-European bank in 1765 by sending his five sons to operate bank branches in the major financial hubs of Europe (London, Paris, Frankfurt, Vienna, and Naples). In those days, banks traded bills of exchange, which were essentially pieces of paper saying the bearer held hard currency at one branch and could therefore withdraw hard currency at another. Trading bills between family members was one way to ensure that fraudulent transactions did not occur. Today, in many countries, family businesses continue to flourish, particularly where the ability to enforce agreements through a court system is weak.

Obviously, the willingness of family members to drop everything to support the new restaurant in the case above is another example of the strength of a family business. The resources of the entire family can be brought to bear on a difficult situation. David could also trust that his family members could run the kitchen and front of house properly. Another benefit was more flexible employment arrangements with family members. "If someone needs a night off or someone's having a hard time, whatever, we've got each other's back 120%," said David. Also, at slow times, it is possible for just the family members to work the restaurant, lowering labor costs significantly. The family also manages to close for a few weeks in the summer for a vacation, something that would be more difficult with permanent employees.

Family businesses also tend to be more stable than traditional firms because so much of the family's welfare is tied to the success of the venture. They therefore do not want to take risks that might threaten

81

the survival of the business and tend to be conservative in growing the firm.

Challenges

David often wishes he had a more traditional relationship with his parents. "You know, go to their place on a Sunday and just relax [but] we're in each other's pockets all the time." Decision-making is also more diffuse, with four family members having to agree on a course of action rather than one CEO. The older members of the family tend to be more conservative in their views making it difficult to undertake new or risky activities. "My biggest issue," said David, "has been trying to go in certain directions with different types of old-school thinking."

Sometimes a family can lack essential skills in a business and need to bring outsiders in. This has not been an issue with the restaurant as all family members are familiar with front and back of house operations. David's early training in accounting also helped to keep the business side functioning. However, in some cases, a reliance on family members to perform key tasks could lead to lower performance if skills were lacking.

Favoritism is also another problem in family business, where family members, however competent, are favored over employees. The new son-in-law being given a vice president's role in Daddy's company is a common trope in film and TV. In fact, the word nepotism is derived from the Italian for nephew, supposedly because some popes gave lucrative positions to their illegitimate sons who they introduced to the Papal Court as their 'nephews.' Competence is obviously an issue, as a favorite may not have the skills or ability to perform in the new role. The morale of non-family members is also affected when they are sent the message that no amount of hard work will earn them a coveted position. Instead, they might end up having to cover for a family member's incompetence.

Succession planning is also an issue in family business. As his parents age and his children grow older, David will have to contend with phasing some family members out and bringing new family members into the restaurant business. The proceeds of the restaurant might only be sufficient to support four adults and thus decisions will also have to be made about the ownership structure and how the profits will be distributed in the future. These can be very challenging conversations to have. According to the Family Business Institute, about 30% of family businesses survive into the second generation, 12% to the third generation, and only 3% to the fourth generation or beyond.[48]

Ways to Develop

In general, David was reluctant to give advice on how to run a family business.

"I'm only talking about my family and every family is different...I don't think you can be prepared enough and you've got to be careful with [advice] because [experience] is the only way you learn. No one gave me any advice. And I think I'm better for it. I think if you go [into business] with a preconceived notion, I've been given this advice that it's going to be like this, and then it's not, it probably could be more damaging."

According to David, learning is key. Things are not likely to work out as planned and you need to pick yourself up and solve the problem. "I mean, there's a small percentage that won't ever fail [and] everything they touch turns to gold and good luck to them. But the vast majority I think, will fail in some way, shape or form. It's not if you fail but when, and then how you respond to that."

David also had some advice on how to deal with decision-making and favoritism. He felt the key to working through key decisions with family members was listening. At the end of the day, people want to feel heard and there is no harm in listening. He felt that if you could put together a solution that shows that you listened to the concerns of others, then discord could be minimized.

Favoritism was also addressed at the restaurant by treating all employees like family whenever possible. "They need to know there is a hierarchy, but that you're on their level," said David. Being seen to perform all of the various functions in the restaurant helped in that regard. "They've got to see you work. And I think if you do that and show them that you're not afraid to work then they respect you a bit more." His family also strives to treat employees as members of their extended family:

> *"Everyone says when they work for us that they feel part of [the family]. They're not on the outside, they're part of it. [We give] them presents for their birthday...nothing big but acknowledging certain milestones because at the end of the day, you're in hospitality, you're in each other's pockets for up to 10 to 12 hours a day."*

George Stalk and Henry Foley, writing in Harvard Business Review, provide some useful advice on how to avoid the traps of favoritism, skill gaps, and succession planning.[49] The first is to avoid saying, "There's always a place for you here." Instead, the family should make sure that only suitably qualified and trained family members are offered positions. They recommend requiring formal training and experience at a non-family firm and a formal competitive selection process.

It is also unlikely that there will be a place for everyone at just one location. Therefore, a family firm has to be willing to grow to accommodate new entrants. David tried to do this when he opened his second location but unfortunately it did not work out. Nevertheless, there will be a limit on the number of people that can be supported at any given location. This limit should not be exceeded. A firm needs to carefully plan for entry and exit decisions, and it might be useful to have an external consultant to facilitate those discussions.

Finally, where possible, new family members in a business should not be supervised by older family members. Instead, the firm should consider appointing a non-family mentor to supervise and guide a new team member. It is recommended that firms also require family members to undergo the same annual evaluations as non-family members so that everyone feels they are subject to the same rules. It also provides an incentive for a family member to meet performance standards and creates room for an improvement plan if targets are not being met. Hopefully, the net result of these tactics will be a strong team of managers who can safely transition the company into the hands of the next generation.

Amy and Thomas are a family business

Thomas and Amy were both well-known figures in the Ruby on Rails software development community when they met in 2006 as fellow speakers at the Canada on Rails conference in Vancouver. Both admitted to being intrigued by the other. Thomas, originally from Vienna in Austria, was a coder. He was best known for his open source Javascript libraries that were used in Ruby on Rails and at large companies like Apple, CNN, and NASA. Amy was a developer, interactive designer, writer, and trainer originally from Baltimore, best known at the time for her cheat sheets about Ruby on Rails. The rest, as they say, is history.

In September 2008 they married, moved to Vienna, and launched a software as a service (SaaS) business named Freckle (now known as Noko). Freckle was devoted to time tracking for developers working on multiple projects for multiple clients, a problem they had frequently encountered in their own consulting work. Freckle billed its first client in January 2009. While they waited for Freckle to build up a client base, they supplemented their incomes with consulting gigs, an e-book on JavaScript, and training. Amy refers to this as 'being your own angel [investor]'.[50]

Now, more than ten years later, Freckle has grossed millions of dollars in subscription revenue, providing an opportunity for the couple to live and travel anywhere in the world. But the money is just a tool for them, enabling them to live according to their primary value, which is freedom. Freedom, for Amy and Thomas, is the ability to control what, how, where, and when they make something, and with whom.

This was a huge priority for the couple. After years of working as software consultants, where bold decisions were often scaled back by risk-averse committees or were never implemented at all, they grew to hate working for others. Their dislike of being an employee or consultant also extended to investors. Taking outside money, they reasoned, just makes you beholden to the desires and timetables of investors instead of employers.

Amy followed on the success of Freckle by creating a training program called 30x500, which teaches others how to experience the freedom that she and Thomas were able to create. The name came from some basic math that Amy had run. In a podcast interview in 2011, Amy says, "I've always been a hustler, I'm always thinking about the numbers." She reasoned that if a business could make $30 per month from 500 clients then a founder could enjoy a comfortable annual income of $180,000, more than enough to buy the freedom to live and work anywhere in the world. Her approach provides detailed step-by-step instructions on how to achieve this goal, an approach she calls 'stacking the bricks,' a metaphor that argues that by laying one brick a day you will eventually build a wall (or house). Freedom then, like Rome, is not built in a day, but by small consistent actions over time.

When asked about the dynamics of working with each other, Amy replied jokingly that, "You can't hire a husband, but you can nag him." Thomas, who admits to being lazy on occasion, also observed that, "It's good to have a team. You can kick each others' butts. Single founders have a hard time motivating themselves." The formula seems to have worked for this couple.

Summary

The term 'family business' covers a huge range of situations. From husband and wife teams, to parents and children, to multi-generational institutions with representatives from three or more generations. The level of involvement can also vary, with some family members being actively involved in managing day-to-day operations, others controlling things indirectly as owners or board members, and still others supporting (or being supported by) the owners and managers.

As we have seen, there are many advantages and challenges to operating a family business. In some ways, these are two sides of the same coin. For instance, the ability to hire family members increases the level of trust and loyalty to the business. On the other hand, it reduces the talent pool, often tempting the family to hire someone who is not qualified for a position. A family business also provides a degree of stability, with the need to provide a consistent flow of income to the family often encouraging a more conservative approach to risk. On the other hand, opportunities may be missed because the family is not willing to risk a large amount of time or capital to pursue something outside its traditional operation. Similarly, the opportunity to work and live together can bring a family closer, but it can also create conflict and a desire for more freedom and independence.

The inherent tensions and contradictions that often arise in a family firm can be overcome and transcended to take the business to the next level of success. Setting performance goals, formalizing selection, conducting training, treating non-family members with respect, planning for the future, and motivating each other to do better are all ways to make this happen. A little bit of professionalism goes a long way.

Small Business Owners

Hillary grew up on the outskirts of Chicago in northwest Indiana, where she graduated from college with a BA in psychology and sociology. After a brief stint in Las Vegas, she moved back to the Chicago area with her husband, son, and newborn daughter. To make ends meet, she took a job at a local office, where she soon discovered she hated working for someone. "I was crying every day the last couple months, and I finally got fired," said Hillary. "So yeah, I need to be my own boss and do things my own way."

This desire to work for herself led Hillary to start a cleaning service in 2003. Initially, she cleaned houses by herself, but soon established a system that allowed her to hire others and scale the business. "I started by myself cleaning one house at a time," said Hillary, "but I knew that I was going to scale it because I didn't want to clean houses, but had to know how to clean houses." Within a year, she had 20 employees working for her.

Unfortunately, the business was hit hard by the global financial crisis in 2008. Hillary lost 40% of her clientele as home cleaning became a luxury for customers who had lost their homes and livelihoods in a scarred economy. Hillary persisted with her business, eventually selling her brand and client list to two of her employees in 2013. "Honestly, I've learned that I'm a good manager," remarked Hillary. "In my cleaning service, I had record retention. I had employees with me for 10 years, which is not common in that industry."

For the next five years, from 2014 to 2019, Hillary was the co-owner of a restaurant and bar in the Old Town district of Chicago, in partnership with her second husband and his parents. Hillary found negotiating business decisions with family members to be challenging, but she was able to apply her leadership and managerial skills from the cleaning business to effectively supervise the restaurant team of cooks, waiters, and bartenders. Hillary is proud of the fact that five of the original staff stayed with the bar during her entire tenure. In her book, low turnover is synonymous with good management. Hospitality is a notoriously fickle industry and it is easy for employees to walk down the road and join another establishment. Hillary is now living in Florida, launching a new venture in catering and event planning, where no doubt her management skills, honed over almost two decades, will be put to good use.

Advantages

There are several advantages to operating a small business that are common with lifestyle entrepreneurs and family business. These include more control over day-to-day decisions, the flexibility to change quickly without layers of approval, and the freedom to create a unique and fulfilling customer experience.

What sets a small business apart from the previous types of entrepreneurs is the focus on hiring non-family employees. The ability to hire good employees is a force multiplier for an entrepreneur. Hillary was able to duplicate her cleaning skills to reach many more clients and make more money. Over time, she was also able to hire an office manager, allowing her to step away from the day-to-day aspects of running the business. Employees can be liberating in this sense.

In other companies, like the restaurant example above, a single entrepreneur cannot perform all functions at the same time, such as waiting on tables and cooking. In the absence of family members, an owner is forced to delegate some of these functions to employees. The economic principles of specialization and comparative advantage are relevant here. Specialization means that some people are just better at some tasks than others. A restaurant owner can cook, but hiring a great chef takes the food offerings to another level. If the extra benefits of having a great chef outweigh the costs then hiring a culinary specialist is a sound decision.

However, it can also be a sound decision to hire someone who is not as good as you at a given task. For instance, I may be a great waiter but an even better chef (i.e. I have a comparative advantage as a chef). As a result, I end up adding more value to the business by working full-time as a chef and hiring a good waiter of lesser ability than working as a waiter myself, or splitting my time between waiting on tables and preparing meals.

Challenges

Why not just hire a great chef and a great waiter? Jim Collins makes the similar point in his best-selling book *Good to Great* where he argues that great leaders should strive to get the "right people on the bus." The right people, in his case, being A-grade players with Ivy league degrees, great attitudes, an impressive resume at other top companies, and a winning smile.

Unfortunately, this is not the reality faced by most small business owners. Instead, there is an ongoing battle to hire the right people, train them, motivate them to give their best, and retain them within the organization. The fact is that A-grade people who *could* work for Fortune 500 companies typically *do* work at Fortune 500 companies.

So, small firms must often choose from B or C employees. The chances of hiring a poor worker are thus higher in small business. The effect of one bad worker is also greater in a small business, because one worker comprises a larger proportion of the total workforce. As a result, small business owners must be willing to identify performance issues early and take remedial action.

Small business owners also find that hiring employees also creates more paperwork. New employees must be verified as eligible to work in the US. Taxes then need to be withheld, unemployment insurance paid, and benefits secured. At the end of the year, employees need to be issued 1099s and W2 forms. Employees also create liability issues, so insurance has to be taken out against errors and omissions and general liability (although this is probably a good idea for a sole owner as well).

Ways to Develop

Hillary credits her success with employees to several factors. First, she is very approachable, and credits her degree in psychology for her philosophy of seeking win-wins instead of taking a "my way or the highway" approach. She also believes in setting firm boundaries. "I feel like a lot of entrepreneurs start their business because it's their passion [and] hire that first person when they're growing and don't think of that part, and then it can get weird." she said. "I've gotten weird relationships where you get very close. And you know, it's almost like I had baby sisters, and then you let them cross a line and then they try to push the line farther." She learned that creating an employee handbook, which outlined rules and standards, was very useful in managing others. "I've had to fire about 20 people in my career," she said. "I'll never forget the first firing. I was so scared. I worked out of my house and wondered what kind of retaliation there would be because they know where I live. They can ruin my business." She found that writing people up for rule violations was tedious but, at the end of the day, she was able to use the documentation to demonstrate a valid cause.

Care must also be taken when selecting and on-boarding people. The selection process can often be improved by writing clear job descriptions, reviewing applications against desired attributes, and asking applicants to give examples of when they demonstrated a particular behavior in the workplace. Once a candidate has been hired, they should be properly trained on the job requirements and the general expectations and norms of the company (also known as its culture). As part of the on boarding process, Hillary also recommends the use of background checks, which are widely available online for a reasonable price. According to Hillary:

> "Background checks are a good hack. You can learn a lot about people with background checks. One time I found a felon and he didn't offer that information to me. Then another time I hired a felon because he did tell me and he worked out. He's still our friend and he's amazing. If you say you're going to run one, too, sometimes they'll give you the information right away."

However, even the best selection process is going to make mistakes and lead to the hiring of employees who lack the requisite skills or motivation to succeed. The restaurant industry uses *staging* (pronounced stazhjing) to counter this tendency. The term is derived from the French *stagiare* meaning trainee or apprentice, and basically involves giving new cooks and servers a test run before offering them a permanent position. Prospective hires work beside trusted employees, who show them the ropes, and verify they have the skills and temperament to handle a fast-paced environment.

Similarly, some firms hire high school and college students as interns (either paid or unpaid) and then offer permanent entry-level positions to the ones that work out. Hillary also used a probationary period of 90 days for both of her businesses, commenting that, "[employees are] usually on good behavior for that first 90 days but they'll usually slip up right before the 90 days. People will show their true colors pretty quickly. So it's easy to weed out those kinds of people."

Of course, internships and probation should form part of a wider performance management system. Management by objectives (MBOs) is the long standing management practice of setting goals for an upcoming period, collecting data on performance, and then reviewing results against target at the end of the period, sometimes tying results to bonuses or other rewards. However, employee performance is such a high stakes issue that it is often better to correct issues, such as tardiness or poor customer service, in the moment rather than wait for an annual review. In fact, in the hospitality industry, failing to show up for a scheduled shift is often grounds for immediate termination under a zero-tolerance policy.

Many business owners have also found promoting from within the firm to be more effective than hiring a senior person from outside. As Hillary puts it, "I don't understand why people hire from outside. I mean, unless there's some kind of amazing leader or someone that has a bunch of accolades, I guess. But yeah, [insiders] already know the culture of the company. They already know your expectations. They already know what's going on."

Hillary also recommends using technology to handle payroll, accounting, and other HR functions. "I love payroll services. It took me two years to convince my mother-in-law to get a payroll service. But I love payroll services. I hate bookkeeping. I hate all that minutiae. So anybody that can help me do that, the better."

Dr. D is an entrepreneur

Dr. Edward E. Dickerson IV (aka Dr. D) graduated from Peekskill High School in New York, before becoming the fourth generation of his family to attend West Virginia State College on a Presidential Scholarship. Following graduation from college in 1988, he was commissioned from the Reserve Officer Training Corps (ROTC) program into the medical branch of the United States Army. Dr. Dickerson then attended the Morehouse School of Medicine in Atlanta, GA.

Dr. D relocated to Fort Sam Houston, TX to complete his surgical internship at Brooke Army Medical Center. Dr. D then served as the 2nd Brigade Surgeon of the 325th Airborne Infantry Regiment in the 82nd Airborne Division at Ft. Bragg, NC, where he earned the coveted Jumpmaster designation. Later he returned to Brooke Army Medical Center to complete additional training in Otolaryngology and Head and Neck Surgery, eventually leading him to serve as the Chief of Staff of Otolaryngology and Head and Neck Surgery at Womack Army Medical Center. While serving his country, Dr. D was recognized with the Meritorious Service Award, Two Oak Leaf Clusters, the Army Commendation Medal, and promotion to Lieutenant Colonel.

After the Army, Dr. D opened his own practice, Cape Fear Aesthetics, in 2004. The practice has since grown to include a rejuvenating med spa, a facial plastic surgery center, and hair restoration. In a newspaper interview with the *Fayetteville Observer* in 2014, Dr. D described "running a small business" as the toughest part of his job.[51] I asked Dr. D about this comment and what made running a small business difficult. He replied that, "When I was making decisions as a Lieutenant Colonel, I was making them for the greater good...you're doing the same thing in private practice, the difference is every decision that you make is connected to your checking account." He went on to say, "the true consequence…is far more than just you getting reprimanded or your boss yelling at you. There is truly a ripple effect that could have an impact over weeks, months and sometimes years. And ultimately, the success or the failure of building wealth for generations."

He initially thought that the transition from the military, where he was responsible for hundreds of employees and millions of dollars, to a small business would be easy. He described the Army as an "obvious food chain of who's the boss and where you are on that food chain. And like it or not, the vast majority of people understand and abide by that food chain. And if somebody gets out alone, it's very easy to take that disruptive link if you will, and remove them from the process." With a small business, "you really do not have individuals who truly understand that particular food chain. And so you have to build that culture, which is a whole lot different than one that's already built for you."

One of the issues that Dr. D found in building a new culture is that you don't have the luxury of hiring the people you want. "You're really a jack of all trades in the beginning and you often can't get the people you want" he said. "You have Cadillac tastes on a Pinto budget." He might list five desired attributes for a position but only get three or four out of five criteria met. "You just need to understand that and if you take the person with two of the five then it's probably not going to be a good decision," he observed. "I had to do more professional development than I ever had to do in the military." Unfortunately, once a person was developed they often went to a higher paying job elsewhere. So, running a practice is a balancing act. Dr. D felt like he was the captain that would go down with his ship if one part of the chain broke. It is certainly the case in a world of online reviews that one bad experience with a staff member can create a negative impression of the business.

So, in the beginning, Dr. D spent far more time on the administrative aspects of the practice than the medical aspects. In most business models many subordinates work and generate revenue to support the boss. This relationship is upside down in medicine, where it is the doctor who is the revenue generator for the practice and subordinates. While employees check patients in, prep them for surgery, and manage billing after a procedure, it is the doctor that is the engine of the company. If the physician is distracted by administrative issues, then the engine slows down. He said he turned a corner when he was able to hire a competent practice administrator. This enabled him to delegate the day-to-day operations of the business to her and concentrate on medicine. "You might have to replace an individual three times before you get it right," he stated. "You have to have the right group of people that understand the culture." He also took steps to systematize his business, relying heavily on the ten Rockefeller habits. "Success is nothing but a habit, and if you create good habits, you can be successful no matter what you do," Dickerson said.

Summary

In this chapter, we explored the challenges of growing a business from a mom and pop operation to an employer. This is a big step that only 25% of startups take. As we saw in our cases, both small business owners struggled to attract, develop, and retain talent. Both Hillary and Dr. D found employees that have been long-time loyal employees, often through a lengthy process of trial-and-error.

Over the years, they also built systems to streamline the management of employees. The ability to delegate day-to-day operations to a trusted subordinate was a major milestone for both of them. We also saw Hillary advocate best practices like background checks, payroll processing, and an employee handbook. Dr. D. found the Rockefeller habits a useful tool.

Hiring employees has the ability to take your business to the next level. Poorly managed employees can also do significant damage to your business, either in lost productivity or damage to your reputation. Successful entrepreneurs must learn to overcome these challenges to realize the benefits that come from leveraging the power of inviting others into your organization.

V

The Growth Entrepreneur

*Growth entrepreneurs seek to grow their companies beyond
the confines of a small business, whether defined in terms of
revenue, number of employees, or profit. When asked, "do
you want to be royalty or rich" the answer is rich.*

Expansionary Entrepreneurs

C hris collapsed on the couch opposite me. His sunken eyes, pallid skin, and general level of exhaustion suggested something was terribly wrong. "How's it going, Chris?" I asked. He confided that he had just opened his tenth real estate office and he was completely swamped. A little more probing indicated that he was micromanaging every aspect of the business in every office. "I sign every check, and approve every sale and listing," he confided. "I just don't trust my office managers to not rip me off. I'm working 24/7 and I'm worried I'll be in an early grave if something doesn't change."

A natural-born salesman, Chris was adept at mounting a charm offensive on any potential buyer or seller. He had parlayed his success in real estate sales to become the managing director of his own chain of real estate offices spread across Melbourne's northern suburbs. It was proving too much for him. "You've really got only two choices," I said, "hire an office manager to handle the paperwork or close down some of your offices."

The next time I saw Chris, several months later, he was back to his old bubbly self. Curious as to how the situation played out, I asked how he was doing. "Oh," he said, "I ended up closing seven offices."

Advantages

Expansion occurs when a firm starts to add multiple locations or products to its portfolio. The most immediate benefit is higher revenues and profits from multiple income streams. If one location can make a profit of $100,000 a year, then ten locations could potentially make $1 million a year for the owner.

Another benefit of managed growth is the growth in customer awareness due to multiple store fronts or product lines. A greater presence makes the brand more visible to the public, driving extra revenue due to word of mouth and a perception of substance. A larger organization is also able to negotiate for better prices from suppliers, and fixed costs can be spread across more unit sales, thus lowering the average cost of each item.

This approach may also be the right path for a founder focused on achieving a significant net worth while retaining control. As we will see in the next chapter, higher growth strategies might require outside funding, which forces the founder to give up some control of the company. In many cases, founders can be forced out as CEO as investors seek leaders who can super charge growth. Founders of expansionary enterprises are more likely to add extra products or locations using retained earnings (or perhaps debt). This means that the company grows more slowly, but control is maintained.

Challenges

As we saw with the case above, there are some challenges with managing growth. The management style that worked at one location might not work well across multiple locations. In a famous article in *Harvard Business Review*, originally published in 1972, Larry Greiner discussed the various crises that arise when organizations grow.[52] He also described the way that these crises could be resolved to allow growth to continue. However, resolving a crisis often requires a revolution in how work is organized in the firm.

The first phase is Creativity, when a company is founded and there is uncertainty about the best products and markets to pursue. The typical startup is pretty laid back with little hierarchy and an 'all hands on deck' mentality that sees people work in different parts of the business as need dictates. A crisis of leadership occurs when a sustainable business model is found and the informal style of the past must be replaced with functional specialists and sound processes. The crisis is resolved when a strong leader is hired (or emerges) to bring order to the chaos, which enables the organization to enter Greiner's second phase known as Direction.

A company in the Direction phase is very centralized. The leader often has to sign off on all decisions. However, as the organization grows, this leads to a crisis of autonomy. The leader becomes overwhelmed with the amount of paperwork and things start to slow down. Business is lost. Frustration mounts. The solution, according to Greiner, is Delegation (his third phase). The leader must update processes and procedures to delegate authority to subordinates. Hence, my advice to Chris to delegate or get smaller.

Delegation, in turn, has its own problems. As Chris identified, more delegation requires trusting that subordinates will do the right thing and act in your (the founder's) interest. Invariably, problems will arise when some of these agents act in their own interests to the detriment of the company. Examples range from minor things, like taking a long lunch, to major issues, like embezzlement. Economists call these 'agency costs.' This leads to what Greiner calls a 'crisis of control.'

Greiner's solution is to enter the Coordination phase and institute more control to limit these costs. In the absence of direct monitoring by the owner, these controls might include incentive schemes, formal planning, budget reviews, time clocks, corporate policies, and new information systems to track behavior and output. In short, all of the features of a major corporation. The risk here, of course, is that an organization will enter a 'crisis of red tape,' where the burden of following all of the rules causes the company to slow down and become less agile.

In Greiner's final phase, Collaboration, the company evolves to work collaboratively in teams drawn from across silos and hierarchies to jointly solve problems. A collaborative firm rewards teams rather than individuals, encourages communication, and creates a culture of experimentation to discover new solutions to difficult problems. In a 1998 update to his original article, Greiner hinted that the next crisis might be a burnout crisis, where the pressure to work on multiple projects and create innovative solutions becomes psychologically overwhelming for many employees. He suggests instituting a period of rest and reflection within and between projects to overcome this tendency.

Ways to Develop

Greiner's framework provides a rich set of ways for founders to develop on a path of managed growth. For over forty years, best-selling author and consultant Michael Gerber has been advising small business owners to "start working on your business, not in it." He argues that the biggest myth in business (the e-myth) is that small business owners are entrepreneurs.[53] Instead, they are 'technicians' who know how to do one thing very well but don't know how to run a business. In Chris' case, he was very good at selling real estate but had little experience in running a multi-location business operation. Gerber argues that a small business owner who wishes to grow must become equal part technician (focused on the product), entrepreneur (focused on vision and innovation) and manager (focused on systems and details).

The secret, according to Gerber, is to stop doing what you do well (working *in* the business) and start building a system that can work without you (working *on* the business). Small business owners often spend 40+ hours practicing their craft and then spend another 40+ hours trying to run the business. As a result, they often end up dreading both tasks as their dreams of freedom evaporate in the face of a tidal wave of work. In another bestselling book, *Rich Dad, Poor Dad*, Robert Kiyosaki points out that financial freedom comes from creating passive income streams.[54] There are only so many hours in the day and only so much per hour that you can charge for your own labor. Passive income, on the other hand, is income you earn indirectly. With a business, passive income comes from the profits that your business generates whether you are there or not.

Seen in this light, Greiner's phases represent different types of systems that an entrepreneur must develop to grow the business in size and sophistication. The processes and procedures developed in the Direction phase solve the crisis of leadership, but this system has to be modified or discarded if the entrepreneur wants to take the business to the next level. The direct control style that Chris developed over time worked well with three locations but started to fall apart when expanded to 10 locations. In this case, a system for delegating authority would need to be created to support the growth.

Gerber ultimately recommends approaching the business like a franchiser (think Subway or McDonald's). This doesn't mean that the business should literally become a franchise. He means that the processes and procedures should be designed so that every part of the organization can be replicated down to the smallest detail. You might have noticed that if you walk into a McDonald's restaurant anywhere in the world, they all have a similar look and feel — the menu, the decor, the pricing, the greeting, the slogan ("I'm lovin' it!"). But the similarities are not just in the customer-facing elements. Behind the scenes, there are also highly specific routines for cooking, cleaning, and employee training. It is this consistency and attention to detail that has enabled McDonald's to grow to almost 40,000 restaurants in 120 countries.[55]

In some ways, this approach is the antithesis of the craft ethos, where every piece of work is unique. There is nothing wrong with wanting to preserve this pride of creation. At some point, however, there has to be some level of systematization if the organization is to grow beyond the founder as technician. Gerber argues that the most successful business owners have this attention to detail (the manager function) as well as a focus on innovation (the entrepreneur function). As we saw in the introduction, Steve Jobs had some brilliant ideas, but he was also obsessive about every tiny detail of an Apple product's design.

Product innovation is about bringing an idea to market, creating new products, features, or services for a group of customers. However, scaling a business is more about process innovation than product innovation. Process innovation is about making a system that delivers value to the customer more effectively and efficiently. There can be just as much work involved in designing, testing, standardizing, documenting, and implementing a new process as in any new product launch.

In the example above, if Chris had decided to keep all 10 locations then he would have needed to implement a delegation system. This might have involved appointing a managing agent at each location to run the office. Processes would need to be developed to hire and train these individuals, set financial targets, and monitor performance. Sometimes these processes can be borrowed from larger organizations in the same industry, but there will also be some fine tuning required to ensure a good fit with the organization in question.

Note that a similar process would be required for a company that expanded its product range rather than its geographical scope. In this case, we would be hiring product managers rather than office managers, but the logic remains the same. Decisions about product pricing, selection, distribution, and features could be delegated to product managers with corresponding protocols for hiring, training, duties, and control.

I would also advise a founder to lay the groundwork to avert future crises. We know that delegation raises agency costs. Therefore, some checks and balances will have to be instituted at the same time that the managers are brought on board. Control systems tend to fall into three categories: output, behavioral, and cultural.

Output controls rely on setting targets. Each office could be required to sell five houses a month for instance. Remedial action could be taken if actual performance falls below target (and perhaps a bonus for exceeding targets). Companies also routinely set targets for expenses through their annual budgeting process, with some sort of review required for unfavorable outcomes.

Behavioral controls involve setting rules on conduct. For instance, a common practice is to delegate a certain spending limit to subordinates (say up to $500) with higher amounts requiring top management approval. This limits the ability for wrong-doing to occur.

Cultural controls are about creating an atmosphere in the company that deters wrongdoing. Emphasizing ethical behavior in the hiring process, conducting training on trust, celebrating employees who 'do the right thing', and having a zero tolerance policy for minor infractions all signal that the company is serious about creating an ethical workplace.

Clearly there are costs involved in implementing these various delega-tion schemes and associated controls. It is important to remember that these decisions should always be taken at the margin, where benefits exceed costs. One of my favorite catchphrases is "perfect is the enemy of good enough." As a company grows, the cost of monitoring every employee also grows. Delegation is then required, which brings its own (agency) costs. Hopefully, the benefits of growth (more revenue and lower expenses) outweigh these extra costs. If not, then something needs to change. However, this does not mean that a small company needs to go out and purchase a $100,000 accounting system when a simple budget on a spreadsheet would suffice. Owners must constantly balance investing for future growth with fixing the problem at hand with the invariably limited resources at their disposal.

This cost-benefit trade-off also sets the limits to growth. As organizations grow larger, adding more locations and product lines, the costs of managing the business also increase. At some point, these costs exceed the benefits of increased size and growth slows or stops. But this limit is not fixed. Process innovations can allow an organization to grow further. As we saw in the chapter on virtual entrepreneurs, information technology has greatly lowered the costs of coordination and cooperation, allowing ever larger organizations (both physical and virtual). However, we are still not at a point where everything is owned/controlled by one large corporation, suggesting that there is still an effective limit to growth.

Brian is an entrepreneur

At the end of his twenty-year stint in the Army, Brian served as the manager for classified command, control, communications, computers and intelligence (C4I) programs for the United States Special Operations Command (SOCOM). SOCOM oversees the various special operations component commands of the Army, Marine Corps, Navy, and Air Force of the United States Armed Forces. In that role, Brian formulated and executed acquisition and contracting strategies for the research, development, procurement, fielding and sustainment of equipment used in special operations of the highest priority and sensitivity. In total, he oversaw the execution of 26 projects valued in excess of $160 million.

After retiring from the Army in 2005, Brian was subject to a cooling-off period where he was unable to work for any of the firms where he had made acquisitions. He decided to leverage his experience by providing advice to companies seeking to do business with the Department of Defense, particularly in classified technology areas. By mid-2005, he had his first contract and, within a few years, the business increased its scope to include technology introduction, training, and sustainment. By 2009, K3 Enterprises had performed work on five continents and, in 2011, the company was named as the 559th fastest growing business in the US by *Inc Magazine*.[56] By 2014, K3 had hit 130 employees and earned revenues in excess of $15 million for the year.

K3's success was noticed by others and its international operation was acquired by a mid-sized defense company in 2016. Brian went to work for the new company as head of its international division and was able to grow revenues from $6 million to $100 million in just 3 years. This also attracted attention and the mid-sized firm was acquired by Huntington Ingalls Industries, a publicly traded Fortune 500 corporation in 2019. Brian now works as the Senior Director for Business Strategy for Huntington but has considered a move back to a more entrepreneurial role once his non-compete period is over.

Surprisingly, when I asked Brian about the secrets of his success, he volunteered that he required every person who consulted him for business advice to read Gerber's e-myth book. He is a big believer in systems and processes. Early in K3's history, with just 18 employees, he sought ISO 9000 certification. ISO 9000 is a quality management system that has historically required extensive documentation of company procedures to assure quality. Many governments require contractors to have ISO 9000 certification to bid for contracts.

Brian saw ISO 9000 as an opportunity to standardize processes across his organization with a policy and procedures manual. "It really made us start looking at our processes," said Brian. "I've seen companies with 200 people, and when they went to ISO 9000, it was painful. Because now that they don't have to change the thinking for 17 other people, they have to change the thinking for 190 other people." As his organization grew, the ISO 9000 certification paid dividends, as new employees could be trained on a consistent set of policies. "Up until [the growth kicked in], we were literally writing programs and plans customized for each one of our customers," Brian commented. "After about 2010…you had to start to making it repeatable…you had to be able to bring project teams in and have the same methodology used each time." As an interesting aside, he noted his Fortune 500 employer had 15,000 ISO policies compared to 1,000 at K3, which reflected the increased complexity of a large corporation, but was also a sign that red tape might be starting to impact the organization.

Brian also attributed his success to several other factors. Knowledge-building was one. When he started ISO 9000 he decided to become a qualified ISO auditor so that he had intimate knowledge of how the whole process worked. Similarly, he worked hard to discover the differences in contracting processes at different federal and state departments. Finally, as part of his standardization drive, Brian also leveraged state training schemes to teach project management, Excel spreadsheets, and process improvement skills to new employees, so that everyone in the company had a common skill set and vocabulary.

Another important factor was finding good partnerships. As his business grew internationally, he found that he outgrew his lawyer, accountant, and banker. He turned to a professional employer orga-nization, called Administaff (now Insperity) to manage the complex tax implications of sending employees to multiple states and countries from several different locations. He also needed to find a larger bank to finance his payroll while he waited for contracts to be paid. He also had to find good employees. Initially, he hired for technical competence in specialist fields, but later he also had to find and retain solid program managers, who could deliver on time and budget without direct oversight. He observed, "If you're having a problem with one of your leaders don't keep them around. You need to get rid of them quick because when you're small, they can do more damage...because when you're small you're basically living on your reputation."

His approach to customers was also interesting. The company never advertised. Instead, it relied on establishing personal relationships. As Brian puts it, "You never buy from your enemies, you buy from your friends, so if you're going to grow a small business you better have many friends." In the early years of his business, he never said "no" to a customer. He always found a way to make things work. However, this was accompanied by a relentless focus on execution. Brian describes his work as "10% plan, 90% execution." His business grew because he developed a reputation for completing tough jobs in difficult places. Eventually, even large companies like Dell Computers were reaching out to him to undertake technical assessments in remote locations around the world.

Summary

Any company that seeks to grow beyond a single location or product will run into some predictable challenges around delegating authority, establishing trust, and ensuring coordination. In some cases, an entrepreneur (like Chris) will decide that the company should stay below this threshold and limit growth. Other entrepreneurs, like Brian at K3, will seek ways to overcome these challenges. However, there is no right or wrong approach on this issue. Growth is not easy and requires major modifications to business operations and management style. It's not for everyone. One of the benefits of being 'the boss' is that you get to choose how your venture operates.

That being said, Michael Gerber's admonition to work on, rather than in, the business continues to be sound advice, as are his subsequent suggestions to create replicable systems for sales, operations, and people management. This work, along with Larry Greiner's information on growth phases, serves to demystify some of the challenges confronting organizations seeking to grow. They provide a road map for what an entrepreneur can expect when they venture down this path.

Gazelle Entrepreneurs

I f you are one of the 4 million babies born in the United States each year, you will be screened for an average of 43 conditions at birth so that early interventions can be taken to save or improve the quality of your life. About 1 in 300 babies test positive for some developmental condition. In the rest of the world, however, over 100 million babies have no access to newborn testing. Thousands of children suffer or even die because of preventable conditions. Rich West and his co-founder, Dr. Vamsee Pamula, created Baebies, Inc. in 2014 with the mission to save lives and make life better for all children by bringing new technologies, new tests and new hope to parents and healthcare professionals worldwide. "The 'e' in Baebies stands for everyone," said Rich, the CEO of the company.

The company started shortly after their first venture, Advanced Liquid Logic (ALL), was acquired by Illumina for $96 million. Baebies licensed ALL's microfluidic technology back from Illumina. The technology allowed them to use tiny samples of blood to run a suite of neonatal tests. The first phase of development aimed to add more tests to the standard panel conducted in the United States. To this end, they started piloting new tests on a proprietary device at three state laboratories and hoped to extend their new protocols to all 50 states. The math was compelling. The cost of testing and early intervention was minuscule compared with the cost of lifelong care for someone with a serious developmental illness. At the same time, the team was also developing a point-of-birth device that could run tests shortly after a baby was born. This product would provide a way to test the millions of children in developing countries who did not have access to a state-funded laboratory service.

Bringing a medical device to market is a hugely expensive undertaking. Technical challenges need to be solved to embed the core technology into a user-friendly device at an affordable price. The device then needs regulatory approval in multiple jurisdictions to verify its effectiveness and safety before it can be sold. Following regulatory approvals, the device must be marketed and then, after a sale, customers must be trained and provided with technical support. A Stanford study from 2010 estimated the cost of bringing a moderately risky medical device to market was $31 million.[57]

Baebies sought to close this funding gap by raising a series of equity injections from a range of funding sources. The first round of priced funding, known as Series A, was closed in July 2015 and raised $13 million. Investors included Rex Health Ventures, the Duke University Endowment Fund (where the original technology was developed), Charlotte Angel Partners, and a loan from the North Carolina Biotechnology Center. This funding was supplemented by a second round, Series B, which raised a further $10 million in October 2017. The new funding was achieved shortly after the company passed a milestone of two million completed tests. At the time, Rich said,

> *"This has been an exciting year for Baebies: our team has grown to 60 talented employees, we have secured FDA clearance for our SEEKER screening platform and we recently announced a global distribution partnership with Labsystems Diagnostics to expand the product offerings in the newborn screening space. We are getting closer to our goal of expanding newborn screening and*

pediatric testing worldwide to the millions of babies that don't have access to it."

Progress has continued unabated since 2017, with Baebies filing for a patent for FINDER, their point-of-birth system, in February 2019, followed by European approval for FINDER in December 2019. The outlook for Baebies looks very healthy, with the newborn screening market expected to grow at 10.7% annually from 2019 to 2026.[58]

Advantages

Taking on venture capital is like adding a booster to a rocket ship. It enables a firm to fly higher and faster than the self-funded approaches we have encountered in previous chapters. In some markets, like biomedical devices, it is often the only way to commercialize new technologies, as banks are reluctant to lend to knowledge industries. Knowledge industries are characterized by high levels of intellectual property and low levels of physical assets, which makes it difficult for them to work with traditional lenders, who typically require some form of collateral that they can repossess and sell if things do not work out.

Venture capital is also well suited to winner-take-all markets that are commonly found in the software industry. Software often costs a lot to develop but requires much less effort to upgrade and maintain. As a result, the profit margins are very high on software once the initial development costs have been recouped, particularly since the internet has made the cost of downloading and hosting software extremely low. At the same time, the leader in a particular software category often captures a lion-sized share of the market. There are many examples that come to mind, including Microsoft Office, Amazon, and AirBnB.

High market shares and high margins translate into huge profits and enormous valuations. A private company with a market capitalization over $1 billion is often referred to as a unicorn. It occurs when a venture capitalist (a VC) buys a part of a company that makes the whole worth $1 billion or more. For instance, if a VC buys 10% of my company in exchange for $100 million in funding, then I have just become a unicorn. In May 2020, more than 400 companies around the world met this definition.[59]

Venture capital firms are thus willing to bankroll promising tech firms at a relatively early stage in order to hit a home run and achieve huge returns for their limited partners, who are passive investors who trust professional managers to place their funds with high-growth companies. Typically, VCs wait for a company to prove a concept in the market and start to scale. They then provide the funds (and often the management team) to accelerate the growth that (hopefully) allows the firm to acquire or maintain a dominant leadership position as the market matures.

These firms are often willing to endure years of losses to cement a leadership position. Amazon, for instance, took 10 years to post its first profit. However, the investors are hoping that the stocks in the company will ultimately be listed for public trading (known as an initial public offering, or IPO) or acquired by a larger player, in both cases yielding early investors a 5x or 10x return on their initial investment. Note that while these returns seem huge, they also have to pay for the investments that don't succeed. In fact, in recent years, the average venture capital fund has failed to meet investor expectations, although the top 25% of funds continue to do well.[60]

Challenges

The first challenge in becoming a gazelle is that venture capital funding is extremely rare. David Rose, managing partner of Rose Tech Ventures and CEO of the funding platform Gust wrote on Quora in November 2015 that 800 companies received Series A funding the year before.[61] That's just 0.03% of the 2.5 million companies founded that year or just over 1% of the 70,000 firms that received some sort of outside seed funding. However, those that received seed funding from a registered VC raised their chances of Series A funding to almost 50%.[62]

Earlier, I used the analogy that VC funding is like rocket fuel. It is also a 'moonshot,' to use another space metaphor. The term has its origins in President Kennedy's announcement in May 1961 that the United States was going to put a man on the moon by the end of the decade. At the time, the technology did not exist and nobody knew how it was going to be achieved, but by 1969 the goal had been reached. A moonshot, then, is a big, hairy, audacious goal that, if achieved, will make a 10x return for investors (when regular investors would be happy with a 10% return). This creates pressure on founders to 'shoot for the moon.'

There is also a high probability that a firm will fail, given the complexities associated with a moonshot. Research firm CB Insights has tracked the fate of 1,119 tech companies that received seed funding from a VC in the 2008-2010 period.[63] By September 2018, they found that 534 (48%) received Series A funding and 335 (30%) received Series B funding. Twelve companies became unicorns with $1 billion valuations. In terms of exits, about 30% of the seeded companies ended up being acquired or going public. Of those deals, 31 were for $100 million or more, and just five were over $1 billion.

A founder is also likely to lose control of the company after taking on large outside investments. Around 80% of venture funded CEOs are ousted by their boards.[64] As we saw in the introduction, Steve Jobs was famously fired by Apple's board in 1985. It is easy to explain how this occurs. The board (of directors) represents the shareholders in a company. Shareholders typically get to elect board members, with the number of shares being equal to the number of votes. Therefore, if outside investors own more than 50% of the (voting) shares then they control the board. The board, in turn, controls the direction of the company by appointing officers (especially the chief executive officer) and determining compensation (among other things). If the board is not happy with the performance of the CEO, then they can vote for a replacement.

Investors use a term sheet to specify the conditions under which they provide money. These terms often include their role on the board, their voting rights, and other protective provisions. These terms are then converted into a shareholder agreement by the firm's lawyers. Clearly, not understanding the terms of a deal can get a founder into hot water, particularly if the details of who will control the company are not well understood. Similarly, the term sheet can also detail how investors can exit the company in the event of a 'liquidity event' like an acquisition or public offering. Not understanding these terms can adversely affect a founder's net worth.

From an investor's perspective, it makes sense to replace the CEO if he or she is not growing the company fast enough. The founder might have excellent technical skills that allowed the firm to reach a certain position in the market, but at a certain point, someone with experience in sales, marketing, and distribution might be needed. Apple brought in John Sculley from Pepsi as co-CEO with Steve Jobs because of his experience in marketing and distribution. He was able to grow Apple from $500 million to $8 billion in sales, but at the cost of losing Steve Jobs when their visions clashed and the board backed Sculley over Jobs. However, within a decade, Apple was facing failure and Jobs was brought back to re-energize the company. In a recent article, Sculley, now in his eighties, described Jobs' insatiable curiosity, perfectionism, missionary zeal, and desire to put a 'dent in the universe' as things he wished to emulate.[65] Often, a hired gun can lack the passion of a founder, and forcing out a founder can have negative repercussions if it adversely affects a company's culture.

Finally, the need to raise multiple rounds of venture capital can also sap the time of a founder. Each round of funding lasts about 18 months on average. Forbes estimates that fund raising can take up to one week a month for six months, from initial introduction to money in the bank.[66] However, some times will be busier than others, and founders will normally have to make several rounds of pitches, answer follow-up questions, and provide data for verification before funds are finally committed.

That being said, the best position for a founder is to have several venture capital firms competing for an investment. Timing a fund-raising round to coincide with a major milestone can be useful in generating a buzz that might translate into multiple funding offers. However, choosing the best deal is not always easy. Term sheets might vary greatly and every VC will tend to offer a compelling package of intangible benefits (many of which should be heavily discounted, according to veteran VC Guy Kawasaki).[67]

Ways to Develop

The first thing to do if you want to raise external funds is to be in the right sector of the economy. Scott Shane, in his book *The Illusions of Entrepreneurship*, estimates that 92% of all VC funding is directed to the information technology and healthcare sectors.[68] Your odds of receiving funding will go up dramatically if you launch in these sectors.

But not every IT or healthcare company receives VC funding. While investors favor companies that solve a big problem in a large market with some sort of proprietary technology, it also helps to have traction. VCs are five times more likely to invest in post-seed companies than pre-revenue startups. Having a great team is also helpful. I like to tell the story of a student group of mine at the University of Texas at Dallas who created the blueprints for a DVD-dispensing machine several years before Redbox came to market. I managed to get them in front of a VC group who politely explained that it was the tenth such proposal they had seen that month.

It turned out that good technology was not enough. McDonald's Ventures incubated the automated kiosk concept, primarily to generate more visits to their restaurants. Rentals of new release DVDs proved to be a popular offering with consumers and Redbox was born. Redbox opened its first kiosk in Denver in 2004, with McDonald's providing the initial locations. Shortly thereafter, Coinstar, which ran coin-cashing machines in supermarkets, purchased a 47% stake in the company. Within five years, Redbox could be found at 42,000 locations, including leading supermarkets, drug stores, and convenience stores, with sales approaching $1 billion. A strong team of founders, partners and advisors with experience in sourcing, operations, and distribution can make a deal more favorable in the eyes of investors.

Finally, not all investors are created equal and founders are often advised to work with investors who bring more to the table than just cash. Finding key executives for a growing company, making introductions to suppliers or distributors, or having a track record of funding multiple rounds are all examples of how a VC can add additional value. If control is important, then founders should push back on terms that might limit their discretion or see them ousted. As with many things, past behavior tends to predict future behavior. Look at how they have treated earlier investments as a guide to how you might be treated. Ask other founders whether the non-financial benefits were provided to them as promised. Check to see if they have a track record of success in funding later rounds and achieving exits.

Igor is an entrepreneur

Venture capital funding for artificial intelligence hit a record of almost $20 billion in 2019.[69] Among those funded was Pryon, an AI company that delivers augmented intelligence for enterprises. Pryon is headed by Igor Jablokov, a Greek-Russian immigrant, who has been working in the voice recognition and AI spaces for decades.

After graduating from Penn State in computer engineering, Igor spent the first decade of his career at IBM, where he led a team working on a project that would become IBM Watson. Watson was the computer that became famous for winning *Jeopardy* against two human champions in 2011. To win *Jeopardy*, Watson needed a module to understand natural language, a technology that was developed by Igor and his team.

In 2006, Igor leveraged his experience at IBM to create a natural language startup named Yap. Yap specialized in converting voicemail messages to text via the cloud, with high accuracy and low cost, replacing human transcribers with machines. It received $1.5 million in seed funding in early 2007, followed by $6.5 million in Series A funding in mid-2008. In September 2011, the tech world was baffled when Amazon acquired Yap for an undisclosed amount. Only later did the world learn that the Yap team had developed the voice recognition technology for Amazon Alexa, the breakout AI product that was launched in November 2014.

Igor founded Pryon in 2017 to bring AI and natural language processing to enterprises to improve how people work. Pryon was the code name for the Alexa project at Amazon. In a recent podcast he outlined his motivation:

"Nobody's gotten through their heads that instead of humans having to learn how to use [computer] systems, we have to conform to the ways that humans are naturally gifted in interacting, and that's through natural language. And so while, you know, Amazon, Google, Apple, and others have been doing a great job in the consumer space, that hasn't been translating to our working life. And so I decided to go take another run at this."[70]

Igor and the Pryon team are developing an AI assistant that uses machine learning and natural language processing to help employees work smarter, make better decisions, and streamline work processes. He cites a recent aha moment when he stopped asking Alexa for things and turned to Pryon's own beta product instead.

To accelerate development, Pryon raised a $4.5 million seed round in November 2018, followed by a $20 million Series A round in June 2019. In another podcast, Igor gave some insights on how he raised such a large amount in a short period.[71] First, he emphasized that past success didn't translate into funding. "It opens more doors and gets you more meetings but it is still a meritocracy where the best business idea wins," he said. Instead, he points to the 6% rule, that you get a term sheet from 6% of investors that you pitch. "So to get 12 term sheets you have to meet with 200 investment funds." Igor argues that this should not be viewed as a complete waste of time, as you get to learn about other companies in a fund's portfolio that could help your business. You also typically receive constructive feedback on your business idea from some very bright people even if they pass on funding.

Igor's seed round was oversubscribed. Initially he was seeking to raise $2 million to fund the company for two years. In doing so, he called on several investors that he had contacted for a potential Series B round for Yap. When they heard about his new company, several were keen to invest. But investors talk, and soon he had other offers turning his round into a 'mango seed' (i.e. a big seed round). He started hiring employees as soon as the first check arrived rather than waiting for the seed round to close. As a result, he already had 20 employees by the time he closed his seed round and started raising his Series A round. Igor doesn't feel bound by conventions like waiting for a round to close or refusing money until you hit an arbitrary milestone.

I asked Igor for some tips on raising funds from investors. He said he learned to focus on the psychology of the deal rather than the numbers, stating, "Venture capitalists are not commodities…money is not money." Each VC brings a different set of expertise to the table in terms of portfolio companies and networks with other companies. Igor calls them superpowers, "Each one of the funds that I selected had its own superpowers that I tapped into." He was also irked by an off-handed comment from a competing CEO that Amazon acquired Yap because it knew it could pay less for a North Carolina company. As a result, he went to great lengths to raise his first money for Pryon from Silicon Valley and sent out his first funding press release from his Seattle office. He also explained that first-tier VCs can be reluctant to invest if they fear a competitor is overly litigious so he consciously seeks to manage the perception that he might be the target of a lawsuit.

In the current environment, Igor doesn't see his funding going towards technology. The cloud makes it easy to scale technology on demand. Instead, the funds are being used to hire the expensive talent needed to stake out a piece of a large market (known as the TAM, or total addressable market). He estimates that the market for artificial and augmented intelligence is currently in the trillions, which is plenty to go around for the relatively small number of players in the space. Igor puts in a lot of hours working to turn Pryon into another success story, often working six days a week, but observes that, "This isn't hard work compared to what our grandparents had to do. I'm just sitting in front of a computer all day."

Summary

This chapter provides some insights into the experiences of gazelles, those high-growth entrepreneurs who seek to super charge the development of their enterprises by raising outside funds. The cases cover health and information technology, the two most common targets for VC funding. Venture financing is not for everyone. Both founders highlighted in the cases were seasoned executives on their second venture-backed business. Both had compelling products designed to serve large markets.

The choice of two firms from my home state of North Carolina was deliberate. This book is based on everyday entrepreneurs in my network. The reality is that venture capital was raised in every state in the union in 2019, although the amounts invested were not equal.[72] West Virginia saw just $200,000 in VC investment, while California received a whopping $65.6 billion. North Carolina was in the middle of the pack, with $1.2 billion invested. By all means, move to Silicon Valley to maximize your chances of investment, but opportunities are also available at home.

In either case, launching a gazelle is going to take a village. You are going to need to form an extensive network of partners, advisors, and mentors if you are going to succeed. In fact, Igor's best advice is to find a CEO who is not a first-time CEO and get mentored by them. In some ways, this is the antithesis of the image of the lone inventor toiling away in a garage, but there is a lot to learn and modern technology changes fast. Keeping your finger on the pulse via the hive mind (i.e. the collective intelligence of your network) is the best way to survive and thrive.

VI

The Super Entrepreneur

Super entrepreneurs operate at the peak of their profession, with net worths in the billions, and are often household names. Only about 600 people are listed as "internet entrepreneurs" on Wikipedia, including such well known names as Mark Zuckerberg and Jeff Bezos. This number is tiny when compared with the 500,000 new businesses that start in the US each month.

Maverick Entrepreneurs

J acque grew up in a small town 30 miles east of Pittsburgh, Pennsylvania, the daughter of a steel worker and a licensed practicing nurse. Jacque reflected on her blue collar background, "People don't make movies, you become a teacher, and you marry the auto mechanic and you work at Denny's...You have a couple kids and you stay put." But Jacque had always felt a little different. Suffering from a form of dyslexia know as dyscalculia, which made arithmetic difficult for her, she yearned for something more. She wanted to make a difference in the world.

Jacque acted on the stage from a young age. After writing a couple of screenplays in high school, she was accepted as a freshman to the Filmic Writing Program in the School of Cinematic Arts at the University of Southern California (USC). While in the program, she won a story development internship with Silver Productions. "I learned how to make films from Joel Silver, who did *The Matrix*," said Jacque. She worked on the scripts for the *Last Boy Scout* and *Hudson Hawk* while she was there.

Jacque acquired the nickname "Maverick," when she turned down an offer for a full-time position at Silver's production company from Barry Josephson, who later went on to produce the Disney movie *Enchanted* and 244 episodes of the TV series *Bones*. "You know what my life plan is," she told Barry, "and it doesn't involve working for

Joel Silver." She even failed a course at USC on practical film making because it did not fit her projected career path. "I want to be a producer. I want to be a writer. I don't want to be behind the camera," she told herself. Eventually, she transferred to anthropology, where she wrote the screenplay for a documentary on studying cultural differences in a futuristic society.

In early 1993, Jacque started her own company, Warrior Entertainment, initially focused on music management. To make ends meet, she started working for a temp agency as an accounts payable clerk. Frustrated with the inefficiencies at her first placement, she quickly discovered that she had a talent for improving accounting and supply chain systems. This blossomed into a full-time career, working in permanent and temporary roles for well-known companies such as Disney, Warner Brothers, and Proctor & Gamble.

But her desire to produce a film remained. In 1998, after a two-year hiatus travelling in Asia, partly working on her Muay Thai kickboxing skills, she started shopping a script for an action movie she had written. The production executives demanded major changes to the script. Frustrated, she decided to finance 85% of the film herself, with proceeds from her now-lucrative consulting practice. She released the feature film, *The Third Society,* in 2002. Problems on the set meant she became the first woman to direct, produce, edit, and star in a feature film. Eighteen years later, she has now produced three more feature films. None of the films have been a financial success, but she has built up a large following under her stage name, J.A. Steel, where she has entries in Wikipedia and the Internet Movie Database (IMDb).

Advantages

In recent years, Jacque has been interested in exploring the role of mavericks in entrepreneurship, culminating in a directed research project under my supervision in 2018. Jacque's research uncovered some interesting facts. The first was that dyslexics are overrepresented among entrepreneurs. Dyslexics make up 5-15% of the general population, but 35% of entrepreneurs are dyslexic, compared with just 1% of corporate managers. Famous entrepreneurs with dyslexia include Richard Branson (Virgin), Ingvar Kamprad (Ikea), and Henry Ford (Ford Motor Company). One site lists no fewer than 22 billionaires with a history of dyslexia![73]

One reason that dyslexics start their own company is because of necessity. Lacking formal qualifications, they often see running a business as the best way to make a living. They also struggle with being labeled a 'loser' in school. Sharon Hewitt, who now owns a relocation company in the UK, was told by a teacher "that if I worked really hard I might be able to get a job as a shop assistant."[74] Barbara Corcoran, of *Shark Tank* fame, similarly remarks that, "I feel like my whole life I've been insecure about looking not smart…everything I do is a constant attempt to prove to whoever's around me that I can measure up." The need to prove oneself is what motivates "a hell of a lot of entrepreneurs to go into business in the first place," she said.[75]

There is also some evidence that dyslexics are better at certain skills, like oral communication, empathy, and non-linear thinking, which help them succeed in business.[76] Struggling with the written word often forces dyslexics to become better at speaking. Similarly, the experience of struggling at school often leads to an ability to identify with the struggles of others. Dyslexics also report that it is easier to see the big picture in a problem and think outside the box because their brains are wired a little differently.

Much has been written about whether great entrepreneurs, like great leaders, are born or made. Part of the problem comes in defining what we mean by a great entrepreneur. In her paper, Jacque viewed an entrepreneur as an innovator, someone who brought something new to the world. This definition favors those who think differently. By this definition, many of the self-employed categories we have explored in earlier chapters would not qualify for the label of entrepreneur. However, if we extend the definition to anyone who receives self-employment income, then we are talking about millions of people, who begin to look a lot like the general population. Similarly, in business, we tend to interpret 'great' in terms of financial success, but even this can be difficult to define. Some studies consider financial success to be turning a profit, while others define success as growth in employees, career satisfaction, or even operational effectiveness.

What do we know about differences between entrepreneurs and the general population, given these qualifications and limitations? First, there is pretty compelling evidence that there is a genetic component to entrepreneurship based on recent twin studies.[77] A twin study compares identical twins, who have the same genes, with fraternal twins, who share 50% of their DNA in common. If genes are *not* important, then identical twins should start businesses at the same rate as fraternal twins. However, this is not the case. An identical twin is much more likely to start a business than a fraternal twin if a sibling has also started a business. And there's more. The rate of business ownership does not change if the twins are raised separately or together, suggesting that a shared home environment is not a large factor.

Gary Vaynerchuk (Gary Vee), a successful social media entrepreneur, strongly argues that entrepreneurs are born.[78] He likens being a millionaire entrepreneur to playing in the NBA. Just as height is a pre-requisite to play at the top level in basketball, he believes that entrepreneurs also have to be born with some inherent talents, including salesmanship, a chip on your shoulder, an independent spirit, understanding consumers, and patience. *"Real* entrepreneurs are born and prove out their DNA with hard work," he says, "What I'm saying is this: only a handful of people have what it takes to truly run a million-dollar business."

So, is biology destiny? I would argue no. First, we do not understand which genes (or combinations of genes) are involved. We are a long way from genetic testing for entrepreneurial ability. Second, even if we could test, there is likely to be a complex interaction between genes and the environment that activates the latent genetic potential. Perhaps an underlying dyslexic condition creates the "chip on the shoulder" that drives an entrepreneur to succeed. The dyslexia, then, is not directly causing the entrepreneurial behavior. Finally, as we have seen with dyslexia, people can compensate for a lack of ability in a given area, either by building a team around them, developing other skills, or working harder to overcome deficits.

Researchers have also been searching for an entrepreneurial personality for decades. For many years, the consensus in academia was there are no common entrepreneurial traits that predict who will start a business or be successful in business. Partly, this was a measurement problem. As I mentioned above, the definitions of starting and succeeding in business vary widely. However, we also know that personality is genetically determined to some degree, so it would be surprising if personality played no role. That being said, entrepreneurship professors have little incentive to turn away students at the door who don't have the 'right' personality. The message that "anyone can be an entrepreneur" is more welcoming, if perhaps a little self-serving. We also need to recognize that personality, like genetic makeup, is not destiny. Entrepreneurs have definitely succeeded without the 'right stuff.'

Even so, there is little doubt that some personality traits are more common in the entrepreneurial community than the general population. Meta-analysis is a research technique that aggregates dozens of studies together, adjusting for sample size and measurement errors, to determine the relationship of one variable to another. A recent summary of five meta-analyses on the personality of entrepreneurs found robust differences between entrepreneurs and non-entrepreneurs.[79]

A common approach is to focus on the 'Big Five' personality factors and compare the scores of (successful) entrepreneurs with managers or other non-entrepreneurs. The Big Five personality traits, represented by the acronym OCEAN, are Openness to Experience, Conscientiousness, Extroversion, Agreeableness, and Neuroticism (sometimes called Emotional Stability). These five factors account for around 50% of the ways people rate personality (using a large number of adjectives). For instance, people who score high on extroversion are more likely to describe themselves as talkative, bold, and energetic, and less likely to say they are shy or quiet. Researchers have found Conscientiousness, Extroversion, Openness to Experience, and Neuroticism to be relatively stable from childhood through adulthood.

Entrepreneurs, in general, are more open to experience, conscientious, extroverted, and emotionally stable than non-entrepreneurs. These broad traits are correlated with the intention to start a business as well as performance after the business has been started. In a recent ingenious study, researchers estimated Big Five traits for every county in the United States using public Twitter data from five million users.[80] These scores were found to predict 30% of the variance in startup activity in a given county, with Openness to Experience, Conscientiousness, and Emotional Stability being the biggest predictors (in that order). Personality was still significant after population density, income, and education level were taken into account.

Other narrower traits have been found to correlate even more highly with entrepreneurial behavior.[81] These traits include: need for achievement, innovativeness, stress tolerance, need for autonomy, tenacity, and proactiveness. Even the simple act of responding faster to an email can be important, as some investors, like Sam Altman, prefer to invest in fast entrepreneurs.

Challenges

Clearly, the biggest challenge presented by the discussion above is whether someone can be a super entrepreneur without the 'right stuff.' What if I'm not dyslexic, don't have the right genes, or fail my personality test? What if I don't have a chip on my shoulder? Does that mean that I will not become a (super) entrepreneur? These are tough questions.

The motivation for this book arose when I asked a panel of three super entrepreneurs at a conference whether they thought entrepreneurship could be taught. Two of them instantly exclaimed, "No!" The third felt that some things could be taught but others were innate (or at least developed at a young age). Derek Jeter, a member of the Baseball Hall of Fame, was quoted as saying "There may be people who have more talent than you, but there's no excuse for anyone to work harder than you do." Gary Vee would argue that if you put in the work (the grind), then talent will determine where you end up. "Learn to love the grind," he says.

But the need to put in the grind also presents a challenge for those that do have the right stuff. They might not put in the work. When Richard Branson left school, his headteacher reportedly said to him, "Congratulations Branson, I predict you will either go to jail or become a millionaire." Dyslexics are more likely to be in prison than the general population. Entrepreneurs are also known to be over-confident and may take excessive risks. As a result, even the most talented entrepreneur may fail to reach his or her potential.

However, success is not assured even when an entrepreneur is a maverick and puts in the grind. Jacque is still waiting to produce a financial or artistic blockbuster despite having put in the grind of producing four feature films. She gave herself until the age of 50 to produce a hit, but is now considering a pivot into a full-time corporate role.

Ways to Develop

The good news is that personality can gradually change over time.[82] Adults tend to become more agreeable, conscientious, and emotionally stable over time. Research also shows that most people want to change some aspect of their personality, with emotional stability and extroversion being the traits most likely tagged for improvement. A recent study found that completing a set of small challenges over the course of a semester could produce changes in reported traits, with the authors of the study stating, "Even small but consistent steps toward pulling one's behaviors in alignment with one's desired traits has the potential to produce trait growth."[83]

This finding is in line with many others who believe that your initial endowments are not fixed. Those with a 'growth mindset' believe that desired behaviors can be practiced and become habits. For instance, the sociologist Daniel Chambliss has written about the 'mundanity of excellence.' After studying Olympic swimmers, he concluded that excellence is mundane and the concept of talent is useless.[84]

"Excellence is accomplished through the doing of actions, ordinary in themselves, performed consistently and carefully, habitualized,

compounded together, added up over time. While these actions are 'qualitatively different' from those of performers at other levels, these differences are neither unmanageable nor, taken one step at a time, terribly difficult."

We can also practice being fast in responding to emails and other requests to satisfy prospective investors like Sam Altman. Tom Bilyeu, founder of Quest Nutrition, counsels aspiring entrepreneurs to ask, "What do my goals demand of me, then work backward to determine the skills you need to achieve them." Similarly, Jesse Itzler, founder of Marquis Jet and husband of Spanx founder Sarah Blakely, has created an entire program around building habits.[85] He encourages budding entrepreneurs to develop 12 habits in 12 months by identifying a deficit or barrier to business success, finding a way to improve on the deficit, and then working for a month to make the improvement a habit or routine.

Daymond is an entrepreneur

Daymond John is the founder of FUBU and an original cast member of the ABC reality show *Shark Tank*. In 2020, his net worth was estimated by Investopedia at $300 million. John did not have a lot of advantages early in life. He was raised by a single mother in Queens, New York and was held back in school. He never attended college. His first business, flipping cars, failed and he ended up working full-time at Red Lobster. Later, he was diagnosed with dyslexia.[86]

Daymond is the epitome of a rags to riches story. He started making his clothing line FUBU (For Us, By Us) in March 1989 by selling hats for $10 a piece on a street corner in Queens. He worked out of his mother's house, with his mom taking out a mortgage on her home to finance the business as the brand started to grow. They were turned down by numerous banks. Daymond is credited with creating the urban clothing segment of the fashion market, a category that did not exist until FUBU came on the scene. The segment is now worth billions of dollars a year and FUBU has grossed over $6 billion in sales in the last 25 years.[87]

He has been asked in several interviews whether entrepreneurs are born or made. He responds that *everyone* is born an entrepreneur, believing that anything is possible, but parents and others distract us by telling us things can't be done. A true entrepreneur is someone who does something they absolutely love. He argues that this explains why many entrepreneurs start their business later in life, when they stop listening to parents and choose to pursue their real passion. John certainly encountered many naysayers in his own neighborhood, and learned to ignore them.

Daymond has written four books, including *The Power of Broke* and *Rise and Grind*. He points out that many successful entrepreneurs, including himself, started with very little and made their fortune. Having few resources forces you to innovate and hustle. Staying hungry as your business grows enables you to adapt to change. People from modest backgrounds also assume they have little knowledge about a situation and therefore are prepared to listen and learn. In *Rise and Grind*, he points out that we all have the same 24 hours in a day. Successful people tend to rise early and go to bed late, working not only harder, but smarter. Like Gary Vee, he believes you need to learn to love the grind, although he claims if someone told him how hard he'd have to work as an entrepreneur, he would have stayed a waiter.

When asked in an interview about his biggest tip for budding entrepreneurs, Daymond replied, "Be decisive." He explains that no-one wants to follow someone who is indecisive. Instead, express confidence and others will follow. He also advocates building a personal brand. "Even when a business goes bad," he says, "people are still willing to follow you if they believe in your brand. Your reputation is something you are developing for your entire life."

Summary

This chapter raises the question of whether you need to be a maverick, or different in some way, to be a super entrepreneur. We learned that some conditions, like dyslexia, are over-represented in the entrepreneurship population. There is also a genetic component to entrepreneurship, and personality differences exist between entrepreneurs and non-entrepreneurs.

We also learned that scientists have yet to isolate an 'entrepreneurial' gene. In fact, contrary to popular opinion, not all entrepreneurs are extroverts. Several well-known entrepreneurs are introverts, including Larry Page, Bill Gates, Warren Buffett, Mark Zuckerberg, and Elon Musk. Nevertheless, it is difficult to imagine someone ascending to the heights of the economy without hard work and a strong need for achievement. Innovation may require an ability to 'think outside the box.'

Risk-averse individuals are also unlikely to take the plunge and go 'all in' on their own business. There is some evidence that entrepreneurs see fewer risks in a situation than non-entrepreneurs. Having parents or other family members in self-employment may reduce the perceived risk of running your own business. So may running a business at a young age. Many entrepreneurs report that they were wheeling and dealing under the age of 10.

Another factor is the lack of options that are available for many prospective entrepreneurs. This may be due to unemployment, a neurological condition like dyslexia, or a prison record. Immigrants may also find it difficult to secure employment in occupations that require formal credentials. These groups tend to be over-represented among entrepreneurs. A rocky start might also contribute to the 'chip on the shoulder' that many successful entrepreneurs credit for their drive to the top.

The good news is that personality traits are not fixed. Habits can be developed and new behaviors acquired over time. While an extremely introverted person may not become a flaming extrovert, he or she can certainly learn to become more extroverted over time, particularly by setting small challenges and acquiring routines and habits. Whether this is enough to overcome the influence of genes, personality, family of origin, and childhood experiences is an interesting question. As I mentioned earlier, many successful entrepreneurs believe they just think differently. If you are intent of reaching the level of super entrepreneur and you do not have these traits, then you probably have some work to do, either by undertaking self-improvement or by assembling a team to compensate for your limitations. Of course, as Daymond point outs, a team also must want to follow you.

Hero Entrepreneurs

E lizabeth Holmes exploded on the scene in late 2013 with an article in the Wall Street Journal and a deal with Walgreens for in-store sample collections.[88] In 2014, she appeared on the covers of *Fortune*, *Forbes*, and *Inc.* magazines as the world's youngest self-made female billionaire. Her company, Theranos, promised to revolutionize blood testing by conducting over 1,000 tests from one finger prick of blood, collected in a 'nanotainer.' Holmes claimed that the idea arose, in part, from her fear of needles. She also spent a summer internship at the Genome Institute of Singapore in 2003 as part of her studies in chemical engineering at Stanford. While there, she observed blood draws from SARS patients and reasoned there had to be a better way.[89]

Holmes returned home to Houston from Singapore and filed a provisional patent in September 2003 for "an ingestible, implantable or wearable medical device" that would detect and treat disease.[90] One embodiment of the idea was a patch that could be worn on the skin, which would painlessly sample bodily fluids through micro needles, direct the fluids to a testing station through microfluidic channels, and then deliver a therapeutic solution. The device would then wirelessly transmit the data back to the patient's doctor.

Arriving back at Stanford for her sophomore year, she shared her idea with Professor Channing Robertson, associate dean of engineering.

Holmes had taken Professor Channing's Introduction to Chemical Engineering class and participated in his seminar on controlled drug delivery devices. Later in her freshman year, she convinced him to allow her to work in his laboratory, and he placed her with a PhD student named Shaunak Roy. She also pitched the idea to Roy who, after graduating with his PhD in chemical engineering, became her first employee at Real Time Cures, later renamed Theranos. Robertson agreed to serve as an advisor and later as a company director.

Holmes had spent part of her childhood in the Bay Area where she was friends with Jesse Draper, daughter of third-generation venture capitalist Tim Draper, whose grandfather had started the first VC firm in Silicon Valley. Draper agreed to invest $1 million in Holmes' startup. Another family friend, Victor Palmieri, also invested, along with Don Lucas, an early investor in Oracle. By the end of 2004, she had raised over $6 million. Unfortunately, at the same time, Roy also concluded that the patch was infeasible, causing the company to pivot towards a hand-held device, much like those used for diabetic testing. By the end of 2005, they had a prototype and two dozen employees.

The company continued to work on perfecting a solution, but creating an accurate, reliable device proved difficult. A demonstration to the pharmaceutical company Novartis in November 2006 produced several errors. There were reports that results on the device before strategic partners and potential investors were 'simulated.' A trial with cancer patients for Pfizer in Tennessee also failed.

Frustrated, Holmes raised more money, almost $30 million. Larry Ellison, the founder of Oracle, was among the investors. The money was used to hire a second engineering team, taking the total number of employees to 70. In September 2007, the new team produced a box about the same size as a computer tower by miniaturizing existing robot and luminescence technology rather than using microfluidics. The new box was given the name 'Edison,' and the original engineering team, along with Shaunak Roy, quietly exited the company. Roy sold his shares for just over half a million dollars.

Theranos demonstrated the Edison device to Novartis a second time in January 2008. All three Edison machines produced errors - mechanical, electrical, and chemical. This was reported back to the board, who fired Holmes as CEO at a meeting in March 2008. However, after two hours of charm and contrition, she was re-instated. A new set of (failed) trials was conducted in Mexico as well as some limited trials with other pharmaceutical companies. The company was quickly running out of money, relying on loans from Sunny Balwani, Holmes' boyfriend, to keep operating. Balwani joined Theranos as Chief Operating Officer in September 2009.

At the start of 2010, the company approached Walgreens and Safeway for the exclusive rights to distribute Edison in pharmacies and supermarkets. Theranos claimed that Edison could run 192 different blood tests, that the system had been validated by 10 of the 15 largest pharmaceutical companies, and that it had been positively reviewed by scientists at Johns Hopkins University. Based on these claims, the companies signed pilot deals worth tens of millions of dollars with plans to launch some customer testing centers in mid-2011.

These deals allowed Holmes to raise a further $45 million in equity funding in July 2010. This raise valued the company at $1 billion, making it a 'unicorn.' However, the reality was Edison was unable to perform all the advertised tests. To cover the gap in testing, Holmes hired another team of engineers later in the year to develop the 'miniLab,' which would be able to perform more tests than Edison.

In 2011, Holmes was introduced to George Shultz, the former Secretary of State, and a fellow at Stanford's Hoover Institute. She promptly invited him to join the board in exchange for shares in Theranos. Shultz was able to influence others to join the board, which ended up including:

- Gary Roughead, a retired US Navy admiral;
- William Perry, former US Secretary of Defense;
- Sam Nunn, a former US Senator;
- James Mattis, a retired US Marine Corps general who went on to serve as President Donald Trump's Secretary of Defense;
- Richard Kovacevich, the former CEO of Wells Fargo;
- Henry Kissinger, former US Secretary of State;
- William Frist, a heart and lung transplant surgeon and former US Senator;
- William H. Foege, former director of the Centers for Disease Control and Prevention; and
- Riley P. Bechtel, chairman of the board of the Bechtel Group, Inc. at the time.

According to John Carreyou of the *Wall Street Journal*, Holmes first met General Mattis in August 2011 at the Marines' Memorial Club in San Francisco. As the commander-in-chief of Central Command, Mattis was responsible for prosecuting the war in Afghanistan. She sold him on the notion of using Theranos to test soldiers in the field. Intrigued by the possibility of saving lives, Mattis ordered a test of the technology. After a lengthy legal review by medical officers, Theranos was warned that the device would probably need FDA approval. Theranos was given permission to conduct a very limited test on non-identifiable blood over a year later. They did not follow up on the offer. This did not stop Theranos from telling potential investors that the machines were being used by the US Army in Afghanistan.

For the next two years, Theranos fought to perfect the miniLab. In the interim, it started testing employees at Safeway headquarters with a combination of conventional machines, using blood drawn from veins and its second device, Edison. Employee samples were ferried across San Francisco Bay to be analyzed at a Theranos lab.

On the threshold of losing the Walgreens and Safeway deals, Holmes decided to come out of stealth mode and launch the company on the public stage. Theranos paid Chiat/Day, Apple's advertising firm, $6 million to launch an advertising and PR campaign centered around the nanotainer, and Theranos announced the deal with Walgreens. With coordinated stories in several influential press outlets, Holmes became the poster child for smart, confident, self-made young women everywhere. In fact, George Shultz referred to her as "the next Steve Jobs or Bill Gates." On the back of the publicity, Theranos was able to raise over $600 million in additional funds, including $96 million from Partner Fund Management in February 2014, giving the company a value of $9 billion. It meant that Elizabeth Holmes was worth $4.5 billion (on paper).

For the next 18 months, Holmes became an A-list celebrity, and started being honored around the country. According to Wikipedia, she:

- was appointed a member of the Harvard Medical School Board of Fellows;
- was named one of TIME magazine's Most Influential People in the World;
- received the Under 30 Doers Award from Forbes and ranked on its 2015 list of the Most Powerful Women;
- was named Woman of the Year by Glamour;
- received an Honorary Doctor of Humane Letters degree from Pepperdine University;
- was awarded the 2015 Horatio Alger Award, making her the youngest recipient in its history;
- was named Fortune's Businessperson of the Year and listed on its 40 Under 40;
- appeared on stage with former President Clinton and Alibaba

founder Jack Ma to discuss "The Future of Equality and Opportunity";

- was named a Presidential Ambassador for Global Entrepreneurship by President Obama; and
- hosted a fundraiser in 2016 for presidential candidate Hilary
  Clinton.

In October 2015, John Carreyou of the *Wall Street Journal* published
the first in a series of scathing exposes on Theranos, based on whistle
blower claims that the technology did not work[91]. Within a year,
the whole shaky edifice had collapsed. Multiple investigations were
launched by federal agencies and charges laid. Lawsuits were also
filed by disgruntled partners, investors, and customers. In June 2016,
Forbes listed her net worth at $0. At the time of writing, Homes and
Balwani are due to face trial on fraud charges in August 2020. The
charges carry a maximum penalty of 20 years in prison.

Advantages

Hero status can be lucrative. There certainly seems to be a correlation
between publicity and fund raising. Elizabeth Holmes first attained
a taste of celebrity at the age of 22 when she was listed as a standout
founder on Inc magazine's "30 under 30" list in 2006, along with Mark
Zuckerberg. Zuckerberg, only three months her junior, was also a
college dropout (from Harvard). The timing coincided with her Series
B funding of $30 million. Seven years later she emerged on the national
stage again in a flash of publicity and raised over $600 million for
Theranos shortly thereafter. The case also demonstrates that hero
status can confer access - access to special events, to other celebrities,
and to awards.

Hero status can also be a form of free publicity. Marketers like to refer to reviews and stories as 'earned media' as opposed to 'paid media.' The right sort of earned media, with a positive spin, can be worth millions of dollars to a company that would otherwise have to generate interest via advertising or promotion. Of course, the converse is also true. Negative media can damage a company, perhaps even fatally.

In their 2010 book *Heroes: What They Do and Why We Need Them*, authors Scott Allison and George Goethals make the intriguing case that people want to be led.[92] Adopting a hero persona may be one way to motivate employees to achieve greatness. Elizabeth Holmes certainly encouraged a missionary zeal among her employees, and dissent was not tolerated. Her staff worked long hours for over a decade in strict secrecy for the most part (as did Holmes). Faith in a leader or cause might be a necessary condition for such dedication.

Challenges

Malcolm Gladwell, in his book *Outliers*, points out that hero entrepreneurs like Steve Jobs and Bill Gates were born at just the right place and time to exploit the microcomputer boom.[93] If they'd been born earlier, then they would have grown up in the era of mainframe and mini computers. Too late, they would have been too young to found companies at the exact time that the growth and interest in microcomputers was accelerating. The accident of being born on the West Coast of the United States and being raised by white, affluent parents also offered them invisible advantages (also known as privileges) that entrepreneurs in south east Asia or sub-Saharan Africa did not have at the time.

Luck often plays a huge role in super-sized success. James Clear, the author of *Atomic Habits*, argues that absolute success is greatly determined by luck, but relative success, how you do against those born in the same circumstances, is a function of hard work and good habits.[94] He argues that hard work allows someone to overcome a bad start or capitalize on a lucky break. There is no doubt that Holmes worked hard. She took no vacations and worked 16-hour days, seven days a week. At the same time, we can recognize her advantage of being born in the United States, to affluent parents, who provided her with a world-class education and social connections that helped fund her startup.

While entrepreneurs can work to shape their hero personas, Allison and Goethals point out that being designated as a hero is ultimately in the eye of the beholder, whether employees, customers, or society at large. At different times in history, different people might be cast as heroes in the popular narrative. In times of war, heroes are likely to be soldiers, whereas in times of pestilence or disease, we tend to lionize doctors, nurses, and scientists. Elizabeth Holmes arose at a time when young women, traditionally under-represented in the ranks of technology billionaires, were looking for role models. This timing no doubt accelerated her rise to prominence. In this sense, attaining hero status is partly a function of the *Zeitgeist,* or the spirit of the times.

Scott Adams, the creator of the *Dilbert* cartoon strip, argues that we often confuse correlation with causation in these matters.[95] As a semi-famous cartoonist, he is often not recognized when he walks into a room. As a result he gets treated like a 'normal' and is perceived to have no charisma whatsoever. However, if people know who he is, then he suddenly becomes the center of attention and people fawn on his every utterance. "Suddenly I have some charisma. I feel like Moses in a room full of water," he says. This suggests that success creates an appearance of charisma and not the other way around. People want to be associated with success. Success breeds success.

Ways to Develop

There is no doubt in my mind that entrepreneurs can craft a hero persona. Allison and Goethals argue that "heroes shape as much as they are shaped...Heroism is based on perceptions of competence and morality, in different combinations for different individuals." At one end of the spectrum are heroes who display great competence - starting a billion-dollar company, inventing a new technology, becoming a world champion. A person can also become a hero by sacrificing for the common good, throwing yourself on a hand grenade or working three jobs as a single mother, for instance. People can easily name their heroes when prompted and one-third of the time, those heroes are family members. Family members are often named as heroes because people are familiar with their struggles and sacrifices.

Hero status is ultimately based on the perceptions of others, and entrepreneurs can work to shape those perceptions, a skill known as 'impression management.' Allison and Goethals refer to the 'Great Eight' traits of heroes: smart, strong, selfless, caring, charismatic, resilient, reliable, and inspiring. Dropping out of an illustrious college like Stanford or Harvard to start a tech firm is a familiar tale. Bill Gates dropped out of Harvard, as did Mark Zuckerberg. Dropping out gives the impression that a) you were smart enough to be accepted, and b) you gave up something of enormous value to pursue an even greater opportunity.

The company received early funding from well-known venture capitalists and was able to recruit seasoned executives to its team while still a startup. This gave the impression that Theranos was a serious operation with serious backers. Even the company's address in Palo Alto signaled that Theranos was a 'serious' company, particularly when it moved to the 'right side of the tracks' several years later.

The careful cultivation of board members by Theranos was also an exercise in impression management. Robert Cialdini, author of the book *Influence*, defines 'social proof' as the tendency for humans to look to others for clues about how to act.[96] Celebrity endorsement is a case in point. If Michael Jordan wears Nike, then they must be the best, and I am making a sound decision by buying Nike. This effect proved equally powerful at Theranos, with seasoned investors and Fortune 500 CEOs neglecting a detailed examination of the company on the assumption that the star-studded board either must have performed the work already, or would not have chosen to be associated with a fraud.

Finally, most observers also agree that Elizabeth Holmes was attempting to emulate Steve Jobs. She dressed in a black turtleneck sweater, adopted a deeper speaking voice for more gravitas, and referred to her system as the "iPod of health care." She also hired former Apple employees and engaged Apple's advertising agency to give her company a similar look and feel to Apple. Her status as a self-made young woman in tech also contributed to her hero status, as heroes frequently need to overcome great obstacles to succeed.

Bill is an entrepreneur

At first glance, Bill Gates appears to be the antithesis of Elizabeth Holmes. Gates is currently the second wealthiest person in the world, with an estimated net worth over $100 billion. The co-founder of Microsoft is now best known for his philanthropic work with the Bill and Melinda Gates Foundation, which operates under the motto "All Lives Have Value." The foundation primarily focuses on preventable deaths among the world's poor. In 2005, he and his wife were named *TIME's* Person of the Year for their charitable work and there is no doubt that his work has saved millions of lives. In addition, Gates set up the Giving Pledge, which encouraged over 200 billionaires to pledge much of their wealth to charitable causes. Warren Buffett, another of the world's richest men, is a noted contributor to the foundation's work.

There are also some interesting parallels between Gates and Holmes. Gates dropped out of Harvard to found Microsoft in 1975. Before dropping out of Harvard, he played in a high-stakes poker game in his Harvard dorm, where he learned the art of bluffing the hard way, by losing a lot of money. His room mate at Harvard, Andy Braiterman, said, "Bill had a monomaniacal quality. He would focus on something and really stick with it."[97]

His bluffing skills came in handy when he and Paul Allen, who had started writing code for local companies during their high school days in Seattle, decided that the release of the Altair computer meant they were missing out on the home computing revolution. Gates called the creator of the Altair, Ed Roberts, to inform him that he and Allen had a BASIC interpreter that would run on the computer. At the time, they had no such thing — it was a bluff. Roberts said he would give a contract to the first person that walked through the door with working software. Gates and Allen launched into a frenzy of activity, building the software in a matter of weeks by emulating the Altair on a Harvard mainframe computer (and earning a reprimand from the Harvard administration). Allen demonstrated the software to Roberts, who agreed to license it, and Microsoft was born.

Microsoft's reputation for vaporware and borrowing ideas did not end there. In 1980, IBM approached Microsoft to license BASIC for their new IBM personal computer. They also needed an operating system. Bill initially referred them to another company, Digital Research, who were not very accommodating. Paul Allen then discovered a small company in Seattle had created an operating system called QDOS. Microsoft bought the rights to QDOS for $50,000 "for whatever usage we wanted."[98] They then rebranded the product as

MS-DOS, selling it to IBM for $80,000, while importantly retaining the rights to license to any other competitor. The PBS documentary *Revenge of the Nerds* described it as "the deal of the century if not the millennium; it was certainly the deal that made Bill Gates and Paul Allen multi-billionaires."[99]

Microsoft Windows, the successor to MS-DOS, was also created after Bill Gates worked with Apple to port Microsoft Office to the Mac. Steve Jobs was furious that Gates had copied his GUI (graphic user interface), but Gates reportedly told him, "Well, Steve, I think there's more than one way of looking at it. I think it's more like we both had this rich neighbor named Xerox and I broke into his house to steal the TV set and found out that you had already stolen it."[100] The judge in Microsoft's antitrust case also noted that the practice of vaporware, announcing products that do not exist and may never exist, was "deceitful on its face and everybody in the business community knows it."[101]

Elizabeth Holmes was thus part of a very long tradition in Silicon Valley of 'faking it till you make it.' Holmes also demonstrated the same level of obsession or focus with her product as Gates. In fact, she toiled for more than ten years trying to realize her vision of a revolutionary way of testing blood. Gates only took a few weeks to develop the first commercial product for Microsoft. In that sense, she was more like Thomas Edison, who famously retorted, "I have gotten a lot of results! I know several thousand things that won't work," when criticized about his failure to develop a new battery. Little wonder she named her second device Edison.

In hindsight, it appears that Holmes set herself a far more ambitious task than Gates. She was warned early on by some faculty at Stanford that her goal of running hundreds of tests from one drop of blood was impossible. But it is also true that people get excited when someone announces an intention to achieve the impossible. Kennedy's goal of putting a man on the moon by the end of the decade seemed impossible at the time. The same could be said about the four-minute mile. The internet is awash with advice to "achieve the impossible." If Holmes had managed to solve the various problems with her device, then there could be little doubt that she would have ascended to the pantheon of the great entrepreneurs. However, at some point, her unshakable confidence (allegedly) turned to fraud.

Summary

A small number of entrepreneurs attain hero status by demonstrating great competence, which is often combined with great sacrifice and the overcoming of great obstacles. This sort of success requires great talent and great perseverance. But luck also plays a role. We have already outlined on several occasions how Bill Gates (and Elizabeth Holmes) had certain advantages by being born in the right place and right time to the right family. Getting a lucky break with an invention also seems to be a prerequisite for success, although innovators do not seem to shy away from borrowing from others when the opportunity arises.

Hero status is also very much in the eye of the beholder. Celebrity entrepreneurs are therefore careful to manage their public personas by projecting certain key attributes to shape their desired images. Even so, there can also a 'halo effect' where attributes like 'charisma' and 'brilliance' are projected onto successful entrepreneurs only after they are successful. Millions of Americans would like to be celebrities and/or change the world. Only a few succeed, and the path to success is littered with the untold stories of those who fell into obscurity, sprinkled with the cautionary tales of those who crossed the line into criminality while trying to achieve the impossible.

VII

The Artificial Entrepreneur

Can computers be entrepreneurial? If so, can we expect them to replace some or all of the functions of human entrepreneurs as the quantity and quality of computer processing continues to grow.

Computers as Complements

Stitch Fix is an online clothing retailer established in San Francisco in 2011. On a regular schedule, typically once per month, they send each of their 2 million customers a box of clothing items that has been personalized for each of them. This personalization considers a number of factors, including personal style preferences, measurements, feedback, trends, season, events (such as a birthday), and budget. Customers get to try on the recommended items, keep what they like, and ship back the remaining items.

The business model earned the company $2 billion in revenue in 2017. What many customers don't realize is that the initial clothing selections are being made by a computer. A sophisticated algorithm selects items based on all known customer information and presents it to a stylist, who reviews the recommendations and makes the final decision on what to ship. The company has named the process 'Hybrid Design.'[102]

In this case, the computer is not just storing and manipulating enormous quantities of data, it is also acting as a decision support tool for the stylist. It is complementing the work of the stylist using artificial intelligence (AI). Early AI (known today as Good Old Fashioned AI or GOFAI) tried to capture domain-specific knowledge by asking experts (such as stylists) to articulate the rules they used to determine an outcome (such as choosing a style for a client). However, expert systems, while competent in narrow domains, were found to lack the nuance and exceptional understanding of seasoned professionals. Experts simply knew more than they could say, something that has been called the 'articulation problem.'

Machine learning is a way of circumventing the articulation problem and underlies much of the excitement in modern artificial intelligence. There are two main approaches to machine learning, supervised learning and reinforcement learning.

In supervised learning, the machine is trained on a set of valid responses to complex stimuli. In the case of facial recognition, a classic use case, thousands (or millions) of pixels from a picture are used as inputs, and the identity of the subject is given as the response. In the simplest terms, the algorithm weighs the contribution of each pixel to a given response. By giving thousands or even millions of examples of these associations, the machine 'learns' the appropriate response without having to elicit every nuance from a human expert.

Stitch Fix uses the feedback from customers to train its algorithm. Success is having a customer keep an item, while a failure is an item that is returned. The machine learns to adjust the weight of each customer's individual preferences and other data to predict which items will be bought.

The algorithm can also generate responses to novel stimuli. This is because it averages the responses from many individual inputs and thus can respond to novel input combinations. The technique is often referred to as 'deep learning' because a number of 'hidden' layers can exist between the stimulus and response layers. These 'artificial neural networks' can aggregate responses from individual inputs in complex ways, and even provide feedback loops, thus mimicking the neuronal structure of the human brain (while also making the underlying logic of a particular response difficult to dissect).

Reinforcement learning, on the other hand, is a technique that allows a machine to learn a sequence of moves over time to realize a goal. The algorithm then observes sequences of moves, either through examining a set of historical games or, more commonly, by simulating many games against itself. Moves that result in large (winning) payoffs receive a reward proportional to their proximity to the final move. For instance, in Tic Tac Toe, there are nine possible opening moves for the first player. If playing an X in the upper right square is more likely to lead to victory, then that move would be weighted higher by the reinforcement algorithm.

The same principle can be extended to more complex games like chess, Go, or online games. It has now been almost a quarter of a century since DeepBlue defeated the world's best human chess player back in 1997. Similarly, AlphaGo was trained in the game of Go and defeated the world champion in 2016. In 2018, a computer was defeating human players on a sophisticated online game called Dota 2, using a combination of supervised learning and reinforcement learning that enabled the machine to simulate 180 years of human game play per day. A similar strategy is used to train autonomous vehicles, which use video of actual drivers and simulated scenarios to gain knowledge of how to react to a range of driving situations.

Advantages

The growth in information technology since the end of the Second World War has been nothing short of remarkable. The first digital computer, ENIAC, debuted in 1946 and was capable of 5,000 addition operations per second (about 1,000 times faster than the fastest human can perform additions). Today, the world's fastest supercomputer, Summit, can undertake a quintillion (10^{18}) operations per second,[103] which greatly exceeds the total processing power of the human brain (estimated at 10^{16} operations per second). Incredibly, scientists working on quantum computing have recently claimed processing times a trillion times faster than Summit for certain problems.[104] Clearly, machines are already superhuman when it comes to raw processing power.

Along with the ability to process vast amounts of data, comes the ability to store and transmit equally large quantities of data. Summit has 250 million gigabytes of disk storage, over 3 million gigabytes of random-access memory, and transmits 200 gigabits of data per second between nodes. And Summit is just one device. Cloud computing, mobile devices, and high-speed networks have made data ubiquitous around the globe. We are now seeing an Internet of Things (IoT) starting to emerge, where household items such as refrigerators, washing machines, and thermostats can collect data and automatically act based on their owners' preferences. Machines can be omnipresent, all-seeing and all-knowing. We have entered the era of 'big data.'

The power of AI to recognize historical patterns enables it to act as a recommendation engine. Consumers are already familiar with companies like Netflix and Amazon providing recommendations based on viewing and purchase patterns. Such approaches can be readily extended to novel applications such as drug discovery or fashion design. If we define an entrepreneur as someone who carries out novel combinations, then these are entrepreneurial acts.

There are three levels of computational creativity: combinatorial, exploratory, and transformational.[105] The first involves finding overlooked combinations of known elements. Computers excel at brute search and can explore every possible combination in a relatively low dimensional space to discover possibilities that may have been overlooked by humans. However, as the number of dimensions increases, there is a combinatorial explosion in the number of possibilities making brute search infeasible. Tic-Tac-Toe has almost 20,000 ways to place an X, O, or blank to fill a 3x3 board. Many of these are not legal states (you can't have all Xs for instance). In chess, with its 8x8 board and 33 pieces (including blanks), the number of possible board configurations is 10^{50}. That's ten followed by 50 zeroes! Again, not all combinations are legal, but the number of possible states has exploded, making the choice of the correct path exponentially more difficult to find.

Exploratory creativity involves searching these higher dimensional state spaces to find novel solutions. Clearly, much of the recent progress in AI has been in this type of creativity, where clever algorithms (and massive computational power) are used to intelligently traverse the state space to (eventually) outperform humans, who typically only explore a tiny fraction of the possibilities that can be considered by a machine.

Once a computer has found an association in the data, it can quickly and tirelessly make recommendations to a human. Every day, Amazon and Netflix present millions of recommendations to their customer bases in real time. In addition to being fast, these recommendations are also adaptive. The algorithm modifies its output based on new data on your habits. Watch a couple of history documentaries and suddenly Netflix shifts its viewing recommendations to more historical content. Buy a book on entrepreneurship and you see a spike in recommendations about similar books you might like on Amazon.

Challenges

The biggest challenge with current AI is the reliance on structured data. Every aspect of a chess game has to be fed into the computer - legal moves, the number and types of pieces, the positions on the board, the objective. The computer has no way to vary these parameters. The third type of computational creativity, transformational creativity, requires a computer to 'think outside the box' and create new elements

- new rules, new pieces, even new games. This is a daunting task that is arguably beyond the capability of any current system. As a result, if the computer doesn't have knowledge on a given aspect of a problem, then it will not factor that variable into its decisions.

Even when a computer stays within the set of given elements, it still requires an enormous amount of data to train it to give the correct response to a novel stimulus. Training often requires thousands or millions of cases to generate enough examples for the computer to create a nuanced response. Nonetheless, some situations, known as *edge cases*, can be so rare that the computer has no historical examples to draw on and thus it reacts incorrectly to the situation. This is not such a big deal when the computer is making recommendations, but is a huge issue if the computer is making the final decision.

As we have seen, neural nets are constantly adjusting the weights of a complicated network of associations to trigger the highest number of positive results. However, the downside of this approach is an inability to describe exactly how it reaches a conclusion. The danger is that the system is only focusing on a small number of spurious inputs to generate a result. This is not a minor concern. Researchers have been able to exploit these weaknesses to 'spoof' neural nets into giving wrong responses.[106] For instance, they discovered that a neural net would consistently label something as a school bus if there were alternating lines of black and yellow. It was not looking for other attributes, just alternating colors. The stakes are not high with school bus identification, but identifying a terrorist or incoming nuclear missile is another matter.

The Uber Tragedy

On March 18, 2018, a tragedy occurred which highlighted the problems using hybrid systems to make decisions. Elaine Herzberg was pushing her bicycle across a four-lane road in Tempe Arizona around 10 p.m. when she was struck and killed by an experimental self-driving car owned by Uber. The accident occurred even though a human safety driver was in the vehicle.[107]

An investigation by the National Transport Safety Board (NTSB) revealed that the computer tagged the bicyclist as an unknown object 6.0 seconds before the collision, while traveling at 43 m.p.h. The computer then determined that the object was a vehicle and then a bicycle. It alerted the human operator 1.3 seconds before the collision that emergency braking was required, but braking did not occur until after the collision. The system did not make an emergency stop of its own accord, as "emergency braking maneuvers are not enabled while the vehicle is under computer control, to reduce the potential for erratic vehicle behavior," according to the NTSB.

The NTSB also discovered that the human operator had been looking down at her lap for 5.3 seconds before the accident and looked up 0.5 seconds before impact. After the crash, police obtained search warrants for the human driver's cellphones as well as records from the video streaming services Netflix, YouTube, and Hulu. The investigation concluded that she was streaming *The Voice* over Hulu at the time of the collision.

For opponents of AI, the Uber case trumpets a clear warning that computers cannot be trusted and the use (or misuse) of computing can have fatal consequences for innocent humans. AI optimists, on the other hand, see the case as an obvious example of human error. If the computer had been allowed to brake, then the accident would not have occurred. In their view, the computer should have had more control, not less.

Summary

Computers are being used every day as decision support tools to support the actions of human operators. The use of these systems has several advantages. They are fast, tireless, and adaptive. They are also capable of finding deep associations in massive amounts of data. At the same time, these systems are fallible. They can only make decisions within the parameters they are given. They are subject to making spurious associations between data, which can be hard for humans to detect, but which can also be exploited by unscrupulous parties.

The bottom line is that computers are subject to error. That error can be in the code, in the logic, or in the interface between the human and machine. As such, they are fine for low stakes operations, where there is human oversight and errors can be corrected quickly and cheaply. High stakes activities, often matters of life and death, are another matter.

As we have seen, computers can be creative in the limited sense of recombining existing elements. Another school of thought argues that entrepreneurs are simply more alert to opportunities than non-entrepreneurs. From this perspective, computers are extremely alert. The Uber vehicle was able to detect and classify the bicyclist much earlier than its human operator by using its advanced sensors. In a less dramatic, but potentially more lucrative application, high-speed trading computers can spot and conduct profitable trades almost at the speed of light.

However, Nicolai Foss and Peter Klein have argued that *judgment* rather than creativity or alertness is the essence of entrepreneurship.[108] An entrepreneur must make a judgment (or decision) on how to allocate valuable resources. Often, these decisions are delegated to managers, supervisors, and employees, or in the case of the examples in this chapter, to a computer. If an entrepreneur is wrong about an allocation decision, including a decision to allocate decision rights to others, then he or she suffers a 'liability of error,' which is typically an economic loss (or, in the case of Uber, a potential criminal penalty). The liability of error, in turn, incentivizes entrepreneurs to be diligent about their decisions.

Foss and Klein call the initial decision to allocate decision rights an 'original judgment' and the subsequent decisions taken by agents of the entrepreneur 'derived judgments.' In the next chapter, we turn to the question of whether computers can ever make original judgments.

Computers as Substitutes

For most laypeople, the thought of machines running the world provokes anxiety. The specter of intelligent machines taking over the world has occupied our imaginations since at least 1863 when the novelist Samuel Butler wrote in *Darwin Among the Machines* that, "…[T]he time will come when the machines will hold the real supremacy over the world and its inhabitants."[109]

Of course, even when Butler was writing in the middle of the 19th century, it was obvious that machines were capable of outperforming humans in a wide range of physical tasks. One of the first applications of the steam engine was to pump water from mines. Thomas Savery, the inventor of the Miner's Friend in 1702, compared the performance of his machine to two horses, inadvertently inventing the concept of horsepower. As horses worked in four-hour shifts, Savery equated his machine to the equivalent of 12 horses (or 120 humans, as a human can only do 10% of the work of a horse).

A century later, the Luddites, a secret society of textile workers, rampaged through central England between 1811 and 1816, smashing mechanical looms and assassinating factory owners. They were protesting the introduction of the power loom, which enabled a factory worker to produce fabric up to eight times faster than a traditional weaver. The notion that we might need to go to war against machines because they threaten our survival or livelihood therefore has its origins at the very dawn of the Industrial Revolution. Fortunately, textile workers were able to shift to other occupations and widespread unemployment did not occur.

In his influential book on the Fourth Industrial Revolution,[110] Klaus Schwab writes:

> *"There are roughly two opposing camps when it comes to the impact of emerging technologies on the labor market: those who believe in a happy ending—in which workers displaced by technology will find new jobs, and where technology will unleash a new era of prosperity; and those who believe it will lead to a progressive social and political Armageddon by creating technological unemployment on a massive scale."*

Schwab goes on to argue that he believes this time is different, with workers facing the threat of being permanently displaced. Those most at risk, according to Schwab, are middle-income knowledge workers whose talents can be learned by machines. Such fears have created a call for universal basic income to meet basic needs, a scheme most prominently championed by Andrew Yang in the 2020 Democratic primary race.

Fortunately, Schwab also believes that "low-risk jobs in terms of automation will be those that require social and creative skills; in particular, decision making under uncertainty and the development of novel ideas." This augurs well for entrepreneurs who excel in these areas because, as we shall see, machine learning is not particularly good at social skills and decision-making under uncertainty.

Dystopian Futures

All of this assumes that the machines will continue to faithfully do our bidding, but dystopian views of technology have outnumbered utopian views by a wide margin. For every Data from *Star Trek*, or Andrew from *Bicentennial Man*, there are seemingly a host of villainous machines, ranging from Skynet in the *Terminator* series, to HAL from *2001: A Space Odyssey*.

HAL and Skynet represent two recurring themes (or motifs) in the stories about dystopian machines. The first of these builds on the realization that a computer can be subject to errors, often as a result of programming contradictions. Jack Williamson's 1947 novel *With Folded Hands* contemplates a scenario where robots have a Prime Directive "to serve and obey and guard men (sic) from harm." This leads the robots to shield humans from all risks, to the point of lobotomizing those who undertake actions the robots deem to be too risky. Similarly, HAL in *2001: A Space Odyssey* decided the best way to resolve the paradox between always telling the truth and being ordered to keep the existence of aliens a secret was to kill the crew. These stories serve to warn us of the dangers of handing complete control over to a machine. Machines may be useful tools that can outperform humans on many day-to-day activities but there are important limitations that we need to observe to ensure that human life is not diminished or eliminated by machine error.

A second concern is that intelligent machines will outcompete us to the point of extinction. Most readers will be familiar with the story of *The Terminator*, where the master computer, Skynet, sends a terminator cyborg back in time to kill the mother of the future leader of a rebellion against the machines. Commentators continue to warn of the existential threat of artificial intelligence, that is, the threat that intelligent machines will take over the world and drive

166

us into extinction as we compete for the same scarce resources. Ray Kurzweil coined the term 'singularity' to refer to the moment when machines become intelligent enough to build even more intelligent machines, thus giving them the capability to evolve into an artificial super intelligence that could threaten us all.[111]

Frankly, I think these concerns about computers taking over the world are overblown. I think the primary threat comes from computers lacking common sense, that is, having lots of specific knowledge but little general knowledge. This, in turn, creates opportunities for entrepreneurs to exploit, increasing their influence on the economy. In the remainder of the chapter, I will discuss the general case against artificial intelligence and the specific reasons that machine learning will not displace entrepreneurs. In doing so, I will throw into sharp relief some of the key characteristics of entrepreneurs that we have explored in earlier chapters.

Advantages

I think the movie *Wall-E* comes closest to depicting a world with widespread machine intelligence. In that world, humans essentially live a life of leisure, waited on by robot servants who undertake all of the menial tasks in society (both physical and mental). Robots cook, clean, serve food, and handle the trash. But they also pilot and maintain spaceships. They are designed to anticipate (and meet) the needs of their creators.

Arguably, this is also the function of an entrepreneur in society, so intelligent machines would make entrepreneurs redundant. Intelligent machines would be able to handle the task of allocating society's scarce resources in an optimal manner. Entrepreneurs would be able to join the leisure class along with everyone else.

Challenges

"It was like claiming that the first monkey that climbed a tree was making progress towards landing on the moon." ~Hubert L. Dreyfus

The late Hubert Dreyfus challenged AI optimists from 1965 until his death in 2017. Writing initially for the RAND Corporation, and dismayed at Herbert Simon's 1965 prediction that AI would be able to do any work that a human could do within 20 years, he quickly identified a glaring weakness in all AI systems. "The basic problem facing workers attempting to use computers in the simulation of human intelligent behavior should now be clear: all alternatives must be made explicit."[112] All current AI systems rely on symbolic logic of the form 'if <these input symbols> then <those output symbols>'. This is true whether we are using expert systems or neural networks. For instance, in the case of facial recognition, the inputs are pixels and the output is the identity of the subject. In the case of a diagnostic expert system, the inputs are symptoms and the output is the name of the disease. Dreyfus argues that while some problems are amenable to symbolic logic, others are not. In general, the more unstructured (or non-formal) a problem the more difficult it will be for symbolic logic.

One aspect of the Dreyfus critique, known later as the 'frame problem,' refers to the difficulty in pre-specifying all relevant aspects of the environment. The philosopher Daniel Dennett humorously describes the difficulties of a robot trying to remove a wagon from a room with a bomb, while not realizing the bomb was on the wagon. A human would have quickly deduced that the location of the bomb was critical to solving the problem.[113]

Melanie Mitchell argues that the computer in this situation lacks 'common sense,' but it turns out that common sense is a complicated matter.[114] There are four types of common sense that humans rely on: physical, biological, psychological, and sociological. Physical common sense refers to our background knowledge about the physical world. We know that an object teetering on a cliff is at risk of falling due to gravity. Our biological common sense tells us that a human will start to get hungry or tired after some time has elapsed, particularly with exertion. Our psychological common sense tells us that a human who is hungry might also become fearful if food is not readily available. Finally, our sociological common sense refers to our background knowledge of social interactions between people. It allows us to discern whether a statement such as, "I'm going to kill you," is hostile or playful. From these examples, it can readily be seen that humans possess a huge array of background knowledge that they can bring to bear on any given situation to make sense of what is going on.

Dreyfus divided the sense-making challenge for a machine into three steps: where to focus, what to focus on, and when to focus. In structured problems, like chess or Go, the computer has been highly focused on a specific domain. Even in the robot example above, we know there is a room with a bomb and a wagon. In unstructured situations, determining where to focus is more problematic. Consider standing watch on a mountain with a 360-degree view to the horizon. Determining which direction to face is a non-trivial challenge. One solution is to focus on everything, but this is not how humans operate given their limited attention spans. We quickly narrow things down to a relevant area of operation. Computers have a much tougher time with this skill (which most humans seem to accomplish effortlessly).

Once we have focused on where to look, we must determine what is essential about the situation. We often conveniently overlook the fact that computers are told what is essential by their programmers but, in an unstructured situation, there is literally an infinite list of relevant factors that could be considered. For instance, consider the room with the wagon. The computer must search its inventory of objects to determine that a wagon exists in the room, that it has functional wheels, that there is an object on the wagon, that the object might be a bomb, and that bombs are not good for the health of the wagon or the wagon operators. At the same time, it must ignore the color of the wagon, the temperature of the room, the sounds emerging from the room (unless the bomb is ticking), and even the number and position of the oxygen molecules floating about the room. While it seems absurd to think that the number of molecules is in any way relevant to solving the problem, it is a very real barrier to a machine that lacks common sense and can simultaneously perceive millions of inputs.

Context is also important. As we saw, the meaning of the phrase, "I'm going to kill you," is dependent on the context in which it occurs. The tone of voice, the proximity of the actors, and the history of interactions all provide clues to interpreting the meaning of the statement. There is mounting evidence that perceptual processing is top down as much as bottom up, meaning the brain forms expectations about what it expects to see from limited sensory data and then confirms its intuition with more sensory data.[115] This enables the brain to economize on cognitive processing by not processing all sensory input.

Normally, there is high fidelity between expectations and reality but sometimes errors (known as 'surprisals') occur between what is expected and received, triggering a search for a more accurate model. So, a statement of hostile intent would normally be accompanied by other hostile actions such as physical aggression or facial grimaces. If, instead, the other party laughs at the statement (a surprisal), then the predictions would be updated to reflect this new information and create a new hypothesis that the statement was said in jest. Additional cues might be used to confirm or refute the new prediction (such as whether the laugh was a nervous laugh or a chuckle).

Imagine, however, if the recipient of the phrase "I'm going to kill you" immediately drops to the ground and starts doing pushups. The brain must activate a wider search of relevant factors to derive an explanation for this unexpected behavior. The next thing that comes to my mind is that the subject might be hypnotized and this is a trigger phrase. But, to the degree that people have different experiences, particularly at the psychological and sociological level, then we would expect them to form different (even competing) hypotheses about what is happening. In fact, the embodiment hypothesis argues that human-like intelligence is impossible without having bodily experiences to ground (or situate) perceptions.

The upshot is perception is an iterative process, and AI models that rely on only bottom-up inputs (like supervised learning) will have a difficult time with ambiguous inputs that require an understanding of context. Using context to decode meaning requires a deep well of common-sense knowledge (and experience) that can be accessed to generate hypotheses or predictions about the world, often by drawing on what Dreyfus calls 'fringe consciousness,' that is, knowledge not immediately applicable to the situation. The human brain is also capable of creating or combining categories to explain phenomena when existing explanations are insufficient. For instance, the term 'iron horse' was used to describe the first steam locomotives in the early 1800s, combining prior experiences of iron and horses into a neologism. As more examples of locomotives proliferated, it became a category in its own right.

Of course, determining what is essential becomes even more problematic when the issue of time is introduced, as the range of possible actions increases exponentially. Games, like Dota, are stretching the limits of computer power by considering 1,000 possible actions per move, 20,000 moves per game, and causal chains of up to 200 moves. Note, however, that this is a formal game where all the possible moves have been pre-specified by the programmers. In the unstructured (non-formal) world, the set of all possible moves is, once again, effectively infinite, making a brute search of all possible combinations of actions impossible (even if all the possible moves could be listed).

Dota also trains its algorithm in a simulated environment that enables it to process millions of possible action sequences every second. Similar simulated environments are being used to train robots and autonomous vehicles. Simulation, however, relies on a detailed understanding of the behavior of the world. In video games, the payoffs from given actions are pre-specified. Damage from attacks with given weapons and the amount of damage a given character can tolerate are easily tracked, along with other critical in-game metrics. In robotic and driving simulations, the programmers can often rely on detailed physical models of the environment. Cars can be taught to avoid objects and robots can learn to manipulate objects. Lessons can then be transferred to the real world. In these environments, so called 'edge cases' loom as a constant threat. These are situations that were not encountered in the simulation, either due to their rarity or non-representation in the simulated world. A robot that has never seen a bomb, has no conception of a bomb, and lacks the set of actions to dispose, defuse, or avoid a bomb will be helpless in the face of such a threat. Similarly, an autonomous vehicle that is unable to recognize a bicycle crossing its path will not react optimally to the situation.

The formal/non-formal distinction acts as a bright dividing line between artificial narrow intelligence (ANI) and artificial general intelligence (AGI). All existing AI is narrow, in the sense that it solves formal problems where the inputs, outputs (actions), and evaluation (payoff) functions are pre-defined by programmers to solve a problem in a specific domain. General AI, on the other hand, must be able to solve problems across multiple domains, by accessing fringe consciousness, making remote associations, solving edge cases, creating new categories, and possessing common sense. In fact, Hintze argues that general AI will only be achievable when a computer develops a 'theory of mind,' that is, the ability to form predictions about the needs and motivations of others. He also recognizes a second level of general AI, which he calls 'consciousness,' where the machine has developed self-awareness of its own needs and motivations.[116]

Such a machine would be able to walk into a room containing a wagon with a bomb on it and surmise that the bomb represented a threat to its own existence and to the well-being of any humans in the vicinity, perhaps by correctly interpreting the expressions of fear on the faces of people staring at the bomb. It might also determine that the bomb will destroy the wagon, which may be of value to another party, and that it might be reasonable to save the wagon as long as it doesn't damage itself or any humans in the process. It might also be aware that it will receive a reward (perhaps in the form of energy) for helping humans.

Clearly, this form of general AI is far removed from the forms of machine learning that we have discussed earlier. Arguably, no amount of training machines on large training sets of actual or simulated data is going to lead to the ability to handle unstructured problems. This will require a theory of mind or consciousness.

Entrepreneurial intelligence

Having established that machine learning is a form of ANI that will not lead to AGI, I will now assert and defend the claim that entrepreneurship is a type of general intelligence and thus not amenable to machine learning techniques. In doing so, I will also refute the claims of AI optimists, who see machine learning as a path to entrepreneur-free economic calculation.

Demand side considerations

The late Steve Jobs is often held up as the epitome of a successful entrepreneur. His founding of Apple, ousting by his own board, and subsequent return to rescue the company and make it the most valuable publicly traded company in the world is the stuff of legend. One of the apparent secrets of his success is a disdain for market research. Walter Isaacson, his biographer, famously quotes him as saying:

> "Some people say, "Give the customers what they want." But that's not my approach. Our job is to figure out what they're going to want before they do. I think Henry Ford once said, "If I'd asked customers what they wanted, they would have told me, 'A faster horse!'" People don't know what they want until you show it to them. That's why I never rely on market research. Our task is to read things that are not yet on the page."[117]

This ability to "read things that are not yet on the page" lies at the heart of the concept of *empathic accuracy*. Empathic accuracy is "the ability to accurately infer the specific content of other people's thoughts and feelings."[118] Jeff McMullen argues that "the variation represented by the introduction of a new product is...speculative in nature and informed to a greater or lesser extent by the entrepreneur's ability to take the perspective of various stakeholders...what is being judged are others' preferences."[119] In the case of Apple, Jobs was able to accurately envisage that products such as the iMac, iPod, iPhone, and iPad would be desired by a sizable number of customers. Importantly, he was able to convince other stakeholders (investors, employees, suppliers, distributors, and contractors) of his vision so that he was able to direct a significant chunk of physical, financial, and human capital to realize his beliefs about customer needs.

Of course, the vision or belief does not need to be 100% accurate. There are numerous cases of companies revising their initial beliefs in the face of feedback from customers or other stakeholders. In fact, obtaining rapid feedback on one's plans is a feature of modern theories of entrepreneurship, such as lean startup and effectuation. As Foss and Klein point out, one of the features of firm ownership is the authority to redirect capital to different activities, which in turn provides an impetus for entrepreneurs to own rather than rent their assets.[120] Companies (and their founders) thus compete on the relative accuracy of their plans and the ability to adjust their plans based on market feedback and the actions of competitors. Empathic accuracy is thus an ongoing process and not a one-shot deal.

Empathic accuracy clearly requires a theory of mind. No amount of information about consumer preferences and buying trends would have enabled an AI to predict the latent demand for the iMac or iPhone. "To infer what product features will resonate with members of a particular group entrepreneurs must simulate (deliberately or automatically) others' decision making by imagining what that target believes and desires," says McMullen. It is therefore an act of 'creative discovery,' which Dreyfus describes as the recognition that a specific solution gratifies a general need. For instance, the iPhone satisfied a need for a technology that was easy to use but that only occurred after the consumer had experienced the device. The genius of Steve Jobs was to recognize that need and present an embodiment of it to the consumer. He was not trying to serve a clearly stated preference. A computer without a theory of mind is thus not capable of evaluating the ability of a specific product to meet a general need.

The ability to combine knowledge across multiple domains is also impossible for a machine that is focused on one narrow domain. Psychologists have described 'conceptual combination' as a fundamental human cognitive skill that combines two disparate concepts together into a higher-level concept. Creative discovery through conceptual combination often involves the engagement of fringe consciousness. Entrepreneurs frequently engage in this process. For instance, the creator of the Lean Canvas, Ash Maurya, recommends developing a high-level concept to describe a new product using a mash-up of previous products.[121] The movie Aliens could be understood as *"Jaws in Space"* or YouTube as "Flickr for videos." Similarly, Scott Shane describes how a single patent was exploited in several different ways by entrepreneurs with different life experiences.[122] He uses the term 'knowledge corridors' to describe how different entrepreneurs will see different opportunities to use a particular technology based on their experiences. Accessing these experiences to combine disparate chunks of knowledge is a very human process.

Similarly, Roger Koppl and his co-authors argue that new opportunities emerge because they are adjacent to new discoveries in other fields.[123] The introduction of fundamental technologies like electricity, steam, and the internet opened an array of opportunities for new products that were not foreseeable before key enabling technologies became available. The success of Amazon, for example, relied not only on the internet but also a capable browser, an electronic payment system, and a delivery service. Opportunities thus unfold over time in an idiosyncratic way that is often rooted in the experiences of individual entrepreneurs. They do not exist in some pre-formed state awaiting discovery via some clever search algorithm.

Supply side considerations

While the successful navigation of consumer demand requires a theory of mind, the investment of one's time, talent, and treasure into a risky new venture also requires considerable self-awareness. According to Hintze, "Conscious beings are aware of themselves, know about their internal states, and are able to predict feelings of others." It is this requirement for a knowledge of internal states that we turn to next.

As we have seen, machine learning requires large amounts of actual or simulated data to drive its recommendations. However, entrepreneurs do not have the luxury of undertaking a brute search of every possible combination to find the best solution. Actions in the real world are consequential. Entrepreneurs have one shot, or at best, a handful of shots to get it right. They live with the possibility of great returns or great losses, including changes in personal fortune, reputation, or even survival. The upside potential, and the downside risk, jointly serve to discipline the entrepreneur to make the best resource allocations possible. Entrepreneurs are making judgments that their actions will lead to success over failure in an uncertain situation and betting their financial and human capital on the outcome.

But what exactly is a machine risking? In a game of chess or Go, the machine has an evaluation function that it is trying to optimize. A successful sequence of moves is rewarded because it moves closer to a pre-determined goal. Similarly, a machine is rewarded in a facial recognition task for correctly matching a set of stimuli to a face. Narrow AI, however, has no concept of existential risk, that is, the awareness that a bad decision can diminish (or even extinguish) one's life. This is what makes an entrepreneur's decisions so consequential. A machine, on the other hand, does not care if a decision leads to its demise or destruction.

For Bert Olivier, care is an essential human trait that distinguishes us from machines.[124] He argues "[machines] cannot die, even if they can be destroyed." As humans, we are aware of our own mortality. We understand the abstract concept of death, and the death of others, but we always live in the shadow of our own demise. This awareness informs our actions. Mortality is part of our "being in the world." or *Dasein.* to use a term coined by German philosopher Martin

Heidegger.[125] We are embedded in the world because of our temporal nature and embodied in the world because of our physical form. We are born, we live, we die. Our experiences from the past, the stories of our ancestors, our present needs for food, shelter, and companionship, and the knowledge that we will die at some unspecified time in the future all inform who we are and what we care about. Machines, at least as currently constructed, have no *Dasein*.

As such, a machine makes a poor entrepreneur because it does not care about the significance of one economic judgment over another. In every AI task to date, the importance of one outcome over another is pre-specified by a human. Humans tell the AI what to care about. We care about winning a chess game, we care about making a profit, we care about not hitting a pedestrian with a vehicle. The AI, on the other hand, places no inherent value on one sequence of moves (or one combination of resources) over another.

The implication is that machines will not naturally demonstrate prudence in assembling resources, having no anxiety (or dread) about negative outcomes. An economy run completely by machines, where machines determine what is valued, would be a disaster. Humans must tell machines what to care about. This prompted Issac Asimov to formulate the three laws of robotics: a robot may not injure a human being or, through inaction, allow a human being to come to harm; a robot must obey the orders given it by human beings except where such orders would conflict with the First Law; and a robot must protect its own existence as long as such protection does not conflict with the First or Second Laws.[126] While other laws have been suggested over the years, the fact remains that there is a void in ethical intelligence that needs to be developed in, or supplied to, machines.

Of course, critics of the free market would argue that entrepreneurs harm humans every day, with Marx famously claiming that profit arises from the exploitation of the proletariat. While not seeking to get into a full-blown debate on the ethics of capitalism, the defense from free market economists is that market capitalism has been more effective in improving quality of life than other forms of economic organization. As Thomas Sowell puts it:

> "While capitalism has a visible cost—profit—that does not exist under socialism, socialism has an invisible cost—inefficiency—that gets weeded out by losses and bankruptcy under capitalism... profit is a price paid for efficiency. Clearly the greater efficiency must outweigh the profit or else socialism would in fact have had the more affordable prices and greater prosperity that its theorists expected, but which failed to materialize in the real world."[127]

It should be noted that entrepreneurs do not just care about profits. They are embedded within a society that sees profit as a means to an end rather than an end in itself. Simply telling a machine to maximize profits is not going to lead to human flourishing. The profit motive in modern economics has been constrained by laws and conventions that have emerged over time to temper the worst aspects of human greed, including prohibitions on slavery, child labor, price gouging, food safety, public health, and monopolies, among others. Knowledge of these institutions, in turn, forms part of the fringe consciousness of every entrepreneur and would have to be incorporated into any AI entrepreneur. Nevertheless, the point is not whether machines can be given an expanded set of rules but rather whether the absence of human emotions (like shame and guilt) and motives (like hunger and pain) make a machine less likely to be a disciplined entrepreneur. I believe this would be the case.

Summary

This chapter raises the simple question, "Can entrepreneurship be learned by machines?" My conclusion is that machine learning, in its current form, is not capable of acting in an entrepreneurial capacity. It lacks a theory of mind and the common sense to anticipate consumer needs. A computer also lacks internal motivations, making it indifferent to good (and bad) choices. While such motivations can be imposed from outside, it will require a sophisticated self-awareness based on the experiential concept of *Dasein* (or being-in-the-world) to navigate unstructured problems with the same assuredness as humans.

Machine learning is still in its infancy and will continue to grow and evolve. However, the machine learning paradigm will not lead to the type of artificial general intelligence popularized in story and on screen. There will still be a role for entrepreneurs and the entrepreneurial functions of empathy and judgment well into the foreseeable future.

Conclusion

The following story is based on the short story "Anecdote concerning the Lowering of Productivity" by Heinrich Boll written for a May Day radio program in 1963.

An enterprising American tourist encounters a fisherman on a pristine beach in Mexico on the fourth day of her five day annual vacation. She decides to observe the fisherman and discovers that he is packing up for the day even though it was only 10 a.m. Snidely she remarks, "You know, if you fished all day you could probably save enough to buy a fishing boat." "And then what," said the fisherman. "Then you'll be able to hire more people, buy more boats, and eventually have a fleet of fishermen who will fish for you." "And then what," replied the fisherman calmly. "Well, then you'll be rich and never have to work again. You can sit on the beach all day doing nothing." "What do you think I'm about to do," said the fisherman, sitting down.

The moral of the story is that work (and money) are simply means to an end. You should think twice before entering the rat race to acquire something that might already be within your grasp. Many of the entrepreneurs that I interviewed valued autonomy and freedom more than net worth. Many of those with high net worths relished the challenge of undertaking larger and more complex projects. The wealth was incidental, more of a scorecard than a goal in itself. Don't get me wrong, material things are nice. But, as the old saying goes, money doesn't buy happiness. Success can only defined by the goals that you set for yourself.

Hopefully, by this stage in the book, you have realized that there are many paths to entrepreneurship and that aspiring to be a billionaire is just one of those paths. Statistics tell us that 40% of American workers will have self employment income at some point in their careers. Exactly what form that experience will take is up to you. In the preceding chapters, I have tried to outline the advantages and challenges of working at different levels. I've also provided a number of hints on how to develop as an entrepreneur at your chosen level.

Of course, there is no law that says you only get to make one choice of entrepreneurial level in your life. As your life and career circumstances change, so to might your entrepreneurial ambitions. Plenty of entrepreneurs, known as serial entrepreneurs, start multiple ventures. They start a company, grow it, sell it, and start again. Their odds of success are higher than someone starting for the first time. Other entrepreneurs are parallel entrepreneurs that have a number of ventures going at the same time. Sometimes it is one large venture and something smaller, and sometimes it is a bunch of smaller things. Once again, there is no right or wrong way to approach the mix of activities that constitutes your entrepreneurial journey.

So, are there any absolutes? Are there common elements that run through every story in this book? I think there are. The first is the need to act. An entrepreneur is someone who *undertakes* something like a project or business, according to the French and Latin origins of the word. The second is that an entrepreneur must have something valuable to exchange. At the end of the day, customers must be willing to exchange money for the product or service that you are providing. To do that, they must perceive that the value they are receiving exceeds the price. Entrepreneurs must therefore possess a degree of empathy with their customers' desires.

A third element is persistence. Amy Hoy calls it 'stacking the bricks.' Laying one brick is not going to make a wall, a house, or even a palace. However, by laying bricks every day, you can eventually create something of great value. A final element is listening. Many of the entrepreneurs in these pages have preached humility. Often, they started out believing they knew more than others in the market. When that did not pan out, they learned to listen to what others were saying and adapt their approach. Sometimes they listened to customers, but other times it was family, employees, investors, and even other entrepreneurs.

While there are some universals, there are some specific competencies that are required at different levels, such as the ability to manage customers, employees, suppliers, and investors as the organization's ambitions are targeted to differing levels of complexity. The chapters on super entrepreneurs also raise uncomfortable questions about whether entrepreneurs are born rather than made - either because of genetic endowments or being in the right place at the right time. We also explored whether entrepreneurs will be replaced by computers. While computers are important tools for entrepreneurs, they are a long way from replacing entrepreneurs altogether, as the unique combination of empathy and calculated risk required to be an entrepreneur is a very human affair.

I like to counsel aspiring entrepreneurs that you do not just show up to the Staples Center and start for the LA Lakers. Professional basketball players have been training for years. Entrepreneurship like anything else requires dedicated practice. The NCAA keeps statistics on the number of players progressing from high school to professional teams. They show that only around 50 (or 0.03%) of 150,000 high school players end up being drafted by the NBA each year.[128] The WNBA drafts about 30 women each year. High school players are seldom compensated for the many hours of practice they put into the game. College players fare a little better, often receiving a scholarship to cover their education.

While many aspire to become super entrepreneurs, the reality is that these people are extremely rare. In fact, the prospects of making millions with a new venture are about the same as playing for the NFL or NBA. And the downside is that your entrepreneurial endowments might just have to be as impressive as the height or strength of a professional sports player to succeed at that level. The good news is that it is not an all or nothing situation. Unlike football or basketball, you can make a good living playing in the minor leagues. And that is *not* OK, it's *more* than OK!

Notes

INTRODUCTION

1 https://www.entrepreneur.com/article/230011

2 https://www.bls.gov/bdm/bdmage.htm

3 https://www.kauffman.org/wp-content/uploads/2019/12/eshipedcomesofage_report.pdf

4 https://www.bls.gov/spotlight/2016/self-employment-in-the-united-states/pdf/self-employment-in-the-united-states.pdf

5 McKinsey Global Institute. *Independent Work: Choice, necessity, and the gig economy.* October 2016.

6 Shane, Scott A. *The illusions of entrepreneurship: The costly myths that entrepreneurs, investors, and policy makers live by.* Yale University Press, 2008.

7 https://howmuch.net/articles/world-map-of-billionaires-2020

8 Shane, *The illusions of entrepreneurship, op. cit.*

9 Global Entrepreneurship Monitor, *GEM Global Report 2019/20* Available at: https://www.gemconsortium.org/file/open?fileId=50443

10 Ibid.

11 https://data.worldbank.org/indicator/SL.EMP.MPYR.ZS?locations=US

INTRAPRENEURS

12 *GEM Global Report 2019/20, op. cit.*

13 Graduate Management Admission Council. *Disrupt or be disrupted: A blueprint for change in management education.* Wiley, 2013.

14 Rauch, Andreas, Johan Wiklund, George T. Lumpkin, and Michael Frese. "Entrepreneurial orientation and business performance: An assessment of past research and suggestions for the future." *Entrepreneurship theory and practice* 33, no. 3 (2009): 761-787.

15 Morris, Michael H., Justin W. Webb, and Rebecca J. Franklin. "Understanding the manifestation of entrepreneurial orientation in the nonprofit context." *Entrepreneurship Theory and Practice* 35, no. 5 (2011): 947-971.

16   Bolton, Dawn Langkamp, and Michelle D. Lane. "Individual entrepreneurial orientation: Development of a measurement instrument." *Education+ Training* (2012).

17   Baker, Ted, and Reed E. Nelson. "Creating something from nothing: Resource construction through entrepreneurial bricolage." *Administrative Science Quarterly* 50, no. 3 (2005): 329-366.

18   Macko, Anna, and Tadeusz Tyszka. "Entrepreneurship and risk taking." *Applied psychology* 58, no. 3 (2009): 469-487.

19   https://www.startupgrind.com/blog/13-ways-to-de-risk-your-startup-failing/

20   Knight, Frank H.. *Risk, uncertainty and profit.* Houghton Mifflin, 1921.

EMBRYONIC ENTREPRENEURS

21   Gartner, William B., William C. Gartner, Kelly G. Shaver, Nancy M. Carter, and Paul D. Reynolds, eds. *Handbook of entrepreneurial dynamics: The process of business creation.* Sage, 2004.

22   Arenius, Pia, Yuval Engel, and Kim Klyver. "No Particular Action Needed? A Necessary Condition Analysis of Gestation Activities and Firm Emergence." Journal of Business Venturing Insights 8: 87-92.

23   Global Entrepreneurship Monitor, *GEM 2003 Global Report.*

24   Liao, Jianwen, Harold Welsch, and Wee-Liang Tan. "Venture gestation paths of nascent entrepreneurs: Exploring the temporal patterns." *The Journal of High Technology Management Research* 16, no. 1 (2005): 1-22.

25   Shane, *The illusions of entrepreneurship, op. cit.*

26   Ries, Eric. *The lean startup: How today's entrepreneurs use continuous innovation to create radically successful businesses.* Currency, 2011.

27   Blank, Steve. "Why the Lean Start-Up Changes Everything." *Harvard Business Review* 91, no. 5 (2013): 63-72.

28   https://patents.google.com/patent/US20170000090A1

29   https://graphics.wsj.com/image-grid/best-of-ces-2018/

EMERGING ENTREPRENEURS

30   Reynolds, Paul D. *Business Creation: Ten Factors for Entrepreneurial Success.* Edward Elgar Publishing, 2018.

31   https://steveblank.com/2010/01/25/whats-a-startup-first-principles/

32   Osterwalder, Alexander, and Yves Pigneur. *Business model generation: a handbook for visionaries, game changers, and challengers.* John Wiley & Sons, 2010.

33   Maurya, Ash. *Running lean: iterate from plan A to a plan that works.* O'Reilly Media, Inc., 2012.

CRAFT ENTREPRENEURS

34   *Self-employment in the United States, op. cit.*

35   Gladwell, Malcolm. *Outliers: The Story of Success.* Hachette UK, 2008.

36   Smith, Norman R. "The Entrepreneur and His Firm: The Relationship between Type of Man and Type of Company." Occasional Papers, Bureau of Business and Economic Research, Michigan State University 109 (1967).

37   Mathias, Blake Dustin. "Wearing Many Hats: Role Identity and Entrepreneurship over Time." PhD, University of Tennessee, 2014. https://trace.tennessee.edu/utk_graddiss/3151/.

38   https://smallbiztrends.com/2019/01/startup-funding-statistics.html

39   Council of Economic Advisors. *The Growth Potential of Deregulation.* Report to the White House. October 17, 2017.

40   Ibid.

41   https://clutch.co/agencies/digital/resources/small-business-digital-marketing-survey-2018

42   *Independent work, op. cit.*

VIRTUAL ENTREPRENEURS

43   https://www.ncta.com/whats-new/a-history-of-speed-as-the-internet-turns-25

44   https://www.publishersweekly.com/pw/by-topic/industry-news/publisher-news/article/81473-number-of-self-published-titles-jumped-40-in-2018.html

45   https://electricliterature.com/everything-you-wanted-to-know-about-book-sales-but-were-afraid-to-ask/

46   Duckworth A, *Grit: The power of passion and perseverance.* New York, NY: Scribner; 2016.

47   https://www.writtenwordmedia.com/100k-author/

FAMILY BUSINESS OWNERS

48   https://www.familybusinesscenter.com/resources/family-business-facts/

49   Stalk, George, and Henry Foley. "Avoiding the traps that can destroy family businesses." *Harvard Business Review* 90 (2012): 25-27.

50   https://stackingthebricks.com/be-your-own-angel-how-to-make-money-happen/

SMALL BUSINESS OWNERS

51   https://www.fayobserver.com/article/20140621/News/306219729

EXPANSIONARY ENTREPRENEURS

52   Greiner, Larry E. "Evolution and revolution as organizations grow," *Harvard Business Review*, July-August." (1972).

53   Gerber, Michael E. *The E-myth revisited*. Harper Collins Publishers, 2005.

54   Kiyosaki, Robert T., and Sharon L. Lechter. *Rich Dad Poor Dad: What the Rich Teach Their Kids About Money-That the Poor and the Middle Class Do Not!*. Business Plus, 2001.

55   https://en.wikipedia.org/wiki/McDonald%27s

56   https://www.inc.com/profile/k3-enterprises

GAZELLE ENTREPRENEURS

57   https://www.massdevice.com/exploring-fda-approval-pathways-for-medical-devices/

58   https://www.databridgemarketresearch.com/reports/global-newborn-screening-market

59   https://www.cbinsights.com/research-unicorn-companies

60   https://seraf-investor.com/compass/article/dividing-pie-how-venture-fund-economics-work-part-ii

61   https://www.quora.com/What-percent-of-start-ups-raise-a-series-A

62   https://news.crunchbase.com/news/the-q4-eoy-2019-global-vc-report-a-strong-end-to-a-good-but-not-fantastic-year/

63   https://www.cbinsights.com/research/venture-capital-funnel-2/

64   https://hbr.org/2008/02/the-founders-dilemma

65   https://www.cnbc.com/2018/05/29/what-ex-apple-pepsi-ceo-john-sculley-learned-from-steve-jobs.html

66   https://www.forbes.com/sites/alejandrocremades/2019/01/03/how-long-it-takes-to-raise-capital-for-a-startup

67   https://guykawasaki.com/the_top_ten_lie-3/

68   Shane, *The illusions of entrepreneurship, op. cit.*

69   https://venturebeat.com/2020/04/14/ai-startups-raised-6-9-billion-in-q1-2020-a-record-setting-pace-before-coronavirus/

70 https://mission.org/podcast/pryon-ceo-igor-jablokov-on-why-the-future-of-work-is-all-about-augmented-intelligence/

71 https://www.youtube.com/watch?v=gLXHec9yPt8

72 https://news.crunchbase.com/news/the-q4-eoy-2019-global-vc-report-a-strong-end-to-a-good-but-not-fantastic-year/

MAVERICK ENTREPRENEURS

73 http://dyslexia.com.au/dyslexic-billionaires/

74 https://www.theguardian.com/small-business-network/2015/jan/15/dyslexic-entrepreneurs-competitive-edge-business-leaders

75 https://www.entrepreneur.com/article/237669

76 https://medium.com/swlh/dyslexic-entrepreneurs-are-successful-by-any-measure-its-all-in-the-way-we-think-9d8ce9562ca3

77 Nicolaou, Nicos, Scott Shane, Lynn Cherkas, Janice Hunkin, and Tim D Spector. "Is the Tendency to Engage in Entrepreneurship Genetic?" *Management Science* 54, no. 1 (2008): 167-79.

78 https://www.garyvaynerchuk.com/the-entrepreneurial-spirit-are-entrepreneurs-born-or-made-2/

79 Brandstätter, Hermann. "Personality Aspects of Entrepreneurship: A Look at Five Meta-Analyses." *Personality and Individual Differences* 51, no. 3 (2011): 222-30.

80 Obschonka, Martin, Neil Lee, Andrés Rodríguez-Pose, Johannes C. Eichstaedt, and Tobias Ebert. "Big Data Methods, Social Media, and the Psychology of Entrepreneurial Regions: Capturing Cross-County Personality Traits and Their Impact on Entrepreneurship in the USA." *Small Business Economics* (2019).

81 Leutner, Franziska, Gorkan Ahmetoglu, Reece Akhtar, and Tomas Chamorro-Premuzic. "The Relationship between the Entrepreneurial Personality and the Big Five Personality Traits." *Personality and Individual Differences* 63 (2014): 58-63.

82 https://pubmed.ncbi.nlm.nih.gov/25822032/

83 Hudson, Nathan W., Daniel A. Briley, William J. Chopik, and Jaime Derringer. "You have to follow through: Attaining behavioral change goals predicts volitional personality change." *Journal of Personality and Social Psychology* 117, no. 4 (2019): 839.

84 Chambliss, Daniel F. "The Mundanity of Excellence: An Ethnographic Report on Stratification and Olympic Swimmers." *Sociological theory* 7, no. 1 (1989): 70-86.

85 https://jesseitzler.com/

86 https://www.lexercise.com/blog/famous-dyslexics-business-and-entrepreneurship

87 https://www.washingtonpost.com/business/on-small-business/when-we-were-small-fubu/2014/10/03/b9280a48-4596-11e4-b437-1a7368204804_story.html

HERO ENTREPRENEURS

88 https://www.wsj.com/articles/elizabeth-holmes-the-breakthrough-of-instant-diagnosis-1378526813

89 The following timeline is drawn from John Carreyrou's 2019 book *Bad blood*, company filings, and https://www.investopedia.com/articles/investing/020116/theranos-fallen-unicorn.asp.

90 Holmes, Elizabeth A., Shaunak Roy, John Howard, and Chengwang Wang. "Medical device for analyte monitoring and drug delivery." U.S. Patent 7,291,497, issued November 6, 2007.

91 https://www.wsj.com/articles/theranos-has-struggled-with-blood-tests-1444881901

92 Allison, Scott T., and George R. Goethals. *Heroes: What they do and why we need them*. Oxford University Press, 2011.

93 Gladwell, *Outliers, op. cit.*

94 Clear, James. *Atomic habits: An easy & proven way to build good habits & break bad ones*. Penguin, 2018.

95 https://www.scottadamssays.com/2013/03/12/managementsuccessleadership-mostly-bullshit/

96 Cialdini, Robert B. *Influence: The psychology of persuasion*. New York: Harper Collins, 2007.

97 https://www.forbes.com/sites/rainerzitelmann/2019/10/28/what-focus-really-means-learning-from-bill-gates-warren-buffett-and-steve-jobs/#191348a473fc

98 https://www.pbs.org/nerds/part2.html

99 Ibid.

100 https://www.folklore.org/StoryView.py?story=A_Rich_Neighbor_Named_Xerox.txt

101 Prentice, Robert. "Vaporware: Imaginary high-tech products and real antitrust liability in a post-Chicago world." *Ohio St. LJ* 57 (1996): 1163.

COMPUTERS AS COMPLEMENTS

102 https://www.forbes.com/sites/bernardmarr/2018/05/25/stitch-fix-the-amazing-use-case-of-using-artificial-intelligence-in-fashion-retail/#1f83cfbf3292

103 https://en.wikipedia.org/wiki/Summit_(supercomputer)

104 https://www.livescience.com/google-hits-quantum-supremacy.html

105 Boden, Margaret A. "Creativity and Artificial Intelligence." Artificial Intelligence 103, no. 1-2 (1998): 347-56.

106 https://www.cs.cornell.edu/information/news/newsitem1271/how-spoof-deep-learning-featured-wired-and-mit-technology-review

107 https://en.wikipedia.org/wiki/Death_of_Elaine_Herzberg

108 Foss, Nicolai J, and Peter G Klein. *Organizing Entrepreneurial Judgment: A New Approach to the Firm.* Cambridge University Press, 2012.

COMPUTERS AS SUBSTITUTES

109 https://en.wikipedia.org/wiki/Darwin_among_the_Machines

110 Schwab, Klaus. *The Fourth Industrial Revolution.* Currency, 2017.

111 Kurzweil, Ray. *The Age of Spiritual Machines: When Computers Exceed Human Intelligence.* Penguin, 2000.

112 Dreyfus, H. L. "Alchemy and artificial intelligence" Rand Corporation, Santa Monica (1965).

113 Dennett, Daniel C. "Cognitive Wheels: The Frame Problem of AI." In *Philosophy of Psychology: Contemporary Readings*, edited by Jose Luis Bermudez, 433-54. New York: Routledge, 2006.

114 Mitchell, Melanie. *Artificial Intelligence: A Guide for Thinking Humans.* Kindle Edition. New York: Farrar, Straus and Giroux, 2019.

115 Clark, Andy. *Surfing Uncertainty: Prediction, Action, and the Embodied Mind.* Oxford University Press, 2015.

116 Hintze, Arend. "Understanding the Four Types of AI, from Reactive Robots to Self-Aware Beings." *The Conversation.* (Nov 13 2016).

117 Issacson, W. *Steve Jobs: The Exclusive Biography.* Little Brown, 2011.

118 McMullen, Jeffery S. "Entrepreneurial Judgment as Empathic Accuracy: A Sequential Decision-Making Approach to Entrepreneurial Action." *Journal of Institutional Economics* 11, no. 3 (2015): 651-81.

119 Ibid.

120 Foss and Klein, *Organizing Entrepreneurial Judgment, op.cit.*

121 Maurya, Ash. *Running Lean: Iterate from Plan A to a Plan That Works.* O'Reilly Media, Inc., 2012.

122 Shane, Scott. "Prior Knowledge and the Discovery of Entrepreneurial Opportunities." *Organization Science* 11, no. 4 (2000): 448-69.

123 Koppl, Roger, Stuart Kauffman, Teppo Felin, and Giuseppe Longo. "Economics for a Creative World." *Journal of Institutional Economics* 11, no. 1 (2015): 1-31.

124 Olivier, Bert. "Artificial Intelligence (AI) and Being Human: What Is the Difference?". *Acta Academica* 49, no. 1 (2017): 2-21.

125 Heidegger, Martin. *Being and Time*. Oxford, UK: Blackwell, 1927/1962.

126 Asimov, Isaac. "Runaround." In *I, Robot*. New York: Doubleday, 1950.

127 Sowell, Thomas. *Basic Economics*. 4th edition. New York: Basic Books, 2010.

CONCLUSION

128 http://www.ncaa.org/about/resources/research/estimated-probability-competing-professional-athletics

About the Author

Dr. Steven Phelan was born in Australia, where he attended Ballarat High School. After graduating with honors from the University of Melbourne, he worked in strategic planning at Telecom Australia and Ansett Airlines. After completing a PhD in computational economics, he held tenure track appointments at the University of Texas at Dallas and the University of Nevada Las Vegas, where he also served as Director of the Center for Entrepreneurship. In 2010, he was recruited to the east coast as executive director of the Center for Innovation and Entrepreneurship at Rowan University in New Jersey, before being appointed Distinguished Professor of Entrepreneurship at Fayetteville State University, part of the University of North Carolina system. While at FSU, he served as fund administrator for a local angel investment group, created a program on business and economic development for the US Army Special Operations Command, and headed the MBA program. As Provost Fellow for Academic Innovation he was responsible for leading a dozen strategic initiatives for the university.

You can connect with me on:

- http://www.drstevenphelan.com
- https://twitter.com/drstevenphelan
- https://www.facebook.com/stevphelauthor

Made in the USA
Columbia, SC
30 June 2021